The
Spiritual
Mandela

The
Spiritual
Mandela

*Faith and Religion in the Life
of Nelson Mandela*

DENNIS CRUYWAGEN

2018 First US Edition

Copyright text © 2016 Dennis Cruywagen
Cover photograph © Jürgen Schadeberg

Originally published in South Africa by Penguin Random House, Cape Town.
This edition by arrangement with VAN AGGELEN African Literary Agency.

At the time of publication, all URLs printed in this book were accurate and active.
Charlesbridge and the author are not responsible for the content or
accessibility of any website.

An Imagine Book
Published by Charlesbridge
85 Main Street
Watertown, MA 02472
(617) 926-0329
www.imaginebooks.net

Library of Congress Cataloging-in-Publication Data Available.
ISBN 978-1-62354-530-7 (reinforced for library use)
ISBN 978-1-63289-221-8 (ebook)

Printed in China
10 9 8 7 6 5 4 3 2 1

*This book is dedicated to the memory of my mother Marie,
her siblings Catherine Louise, Wallace, and Melvyn, the first people
to introduce me to the absolute joy of reading.
It is also in remembrance of my father Henry, an illiterate man
who slaved to give his children the education he did not have.*

Contents

Acknowledgments.. ix

Introduction.. 1

1. Spiritual Origins... 9

2. A Methodist Education................................... 21

3. The Runaway 35

4. Politics, Before Anything Else 45

5. Taking Up Arms 65

6. An Imprisonment of the Spirit...................... 79

7. The Sacrament Behind Bars 99

8. Confessions of Faith.................................... 123

9. A Transcendental Leader 147

10. Last Rites 171

Conclusion 189

Notes 195

Bibliography.. 211

Index... 219

Acknowledgments

Writing a book of this nature has required me to travel to different parts of South Africa, and the support I received from friends and family who assisted me with accommodation and getting around in strange, unfamiliar places was essential in this regard. My sincere gratitude goes to Monty and Antoinetta Breytenbach, Magda Greyling, Justice and Carol Hofmeyr, Ruben Louw and Fred van der Linde.

For support, cajoling and pep talks, thank you to Professor Henry Bredekamp, my siblings Bennie, Roy, Vincent, Colin, Cheryl and Andre, and my sister-in-law Lebo Cruywagen.

Also deepest thanks to John and Lynn Bowles, Liezil Cerf, Jan and the late Toekie de Necker, Asa Kamalie-Fernold, Nicki Fourie, Sam Henkeman, Linda Jacobs, Ayjay and Maggie Jantjies, Anchen Knoblauch, Obie Labuschagne, the Manthatha family, Sharon May, Segun and Rachel Olipekun, Judith Roberts, Lionel and Rose Roode, Hannelie Smit, Maimie Steenkamp, Ted Thorpe, Siobhan Tregoning, Siviwe Tukwayo, Ina van Staden, Marietjie van Zyl, that ebullient raconteur and journalist Paul Vecchiatto, the indomitable Johanna Viljoen, and Ricardo Wessels.

To Colleen Sables (née Brink), who I have known since primary school when we used to play our own version of football in Heideveld: thank you for the years of support and encouragement.

I'm also grateful to Verne Harris and Sahm Venter of the

Nelson Mandela Foundation for often pointing me in the right direction during my research, and to Natalie Skomolo and her colleagues at the National Archives for being so helpful and accommodating.

At Penguin Random House, thank you to Robert Plummer and Marlene Fryer for believing in this book from the start, and for your faith, patience and confidence. Genevieve Adams added finesse during the editing of this book, which greatly improved it.

Thank you as well to the numerous individuals who I interviewed for this book. Your willingness to allow me to take a glimpse into your chest of memories and hear your precious stories was a gift.

Special thanks to the loyal Louise Korentajer, to my friend, comrade and sister Ayesha Ismail, and to Patricia de Lille. Most of all, thank you to Lianda.

DENNIS CRUYWAGEN
AUGUST 2016

Introduction

T HE LIFE OF Nelson Mandela has been studied in almost exhaustive detail. Countless books, articles, television documentaries, films, websites and school essays have attempted to understand how a boy from rural Transkei in the Eastern Cape could grow up to become the first black president of democratic South Africa. Many accounts rightly attribute Mandela's achievements to the extraordinary amount of courage and perseverance he displayed throughout the years he fought in the struggle against apartheid, and during the long and isolating years of his imprisonment. However, there was also another side to Mandela, one that is rarely referenced in any narrative about his life, but which nevertheless played an integral role in shaping the man that he was to become. While he never revealed it publicly, and only rarely referred to it in private to individuals outside of his family and close circle of friends, Mandela's spirituality and the Methodist beliefs he adopted in childhood were inseparable aspects of his character, and went a long way towards informing his personal philosophy and some of his most important political decisions.

For obvious reasons, Mandela's political career dominates the majority of discussions about his life. Politics and his commitment to his political party, the African National Congress (ANC), consumed most of Mandela's existence before his imprisonment on Robben Island, and influenced the way other people thought of him or understood him. For many years, to both black and white South Africans, he was, before anything else, Nelson Mandela the political activist, the man who was prepared to give up his life in the fight for black South Africans' freedom. The inherent righteousness of his cause, upon which depended the lives of millions of people, justified this intense devotion to politics and Mandela's reasoning for putting it first in his life, even if this meant that both his faith and his family suffered as a result. It also fostered a sense of pragmatism in him, which helped to propel his commitment to the armed struggle, even when other prominent members of the ANC, such as the organization's president, Albert Luthuli, voiced Christian concerns about using force to accelerate the resistance campaign.

Adding to the lack of awareness about Mandela's deep spiritual beliefs was his twenty-seven-year-long imprisonment after the life sentence he received in the Rivonia Trial. This was despite the fact that his religious beliefs would grow stronger in the eighteen years he spent on Robben Island, where he was, according to his own admission, "quite religious."[1] The prospect of spending the rest of his life on Robben Island no doubt worked towards developing his spiritual awareness, and religion became an effective and positive means of coping with the hardships he endured there. Even so, the isolation in which he and his fellow political prisoners were kept provided the apartheid state with an opportunity to advance an image of them that was in keeping with the type of Cold War propaganda that circulated at that time, when anyone who questioned or threatened the laws underpinning a Western rule of government was immediately branded an enemy of the state. In such context,

Mandela's opposition to apartheid automatically implied that he was both a communist and anathema to Western ideology and the beliefs that upheld it, including Christianity. But while the South African Communist Party (SACP) claims that Mandela was a member for a brief period, in 1962, this clearly did not prevent him, based on his own testimony and that of his fellow inmates, from participating in religious services during his imprisonment, or from interacting with ministers from a number of churches.[2] To many white South Africans at the time, however, the thought of even placing Mandela's name next to the word "spiritual" would have been a laughable or absurd notion.

Finally, there is the contribution, or lack thereof, that Mandela himself made towards the small body of knowledge that examines his religious beliefs. As mentioned before, Mandela was too pre-occupied by political concerns during the struggle to place any special emphasis on his faith in directing the path he took towards obtaining racial equality, although he did see the value of utilizing church support in advocating the cause among its followers. After his release from prison in 1990, Mandela hardly ever spoke about his religious beliefs in public or to the media. In an interview with Charles Villa-Vicencio in the early 1990s, before he was elected president, Mandela, when asked about whether he considered himself a religious person, denied it: "No, I am not particularly religious or spiritual. Let's say I am interested in all attempts to discover the meaning and purpose of life. Religion is an important part of this exercise."[3]

While this statement could be taken as definitive proof of Mandela's religious outlook, it also contradicts the accounts of a number of people who got to know him while he was in prison and after his release, and who contend that he was indeed a deeply spiritual person whose faith formed the foundation of his policy of reconciliation after his election as president in 1994. Some of these witnesses include Mandela's personal chaplain, Methodist bishop Don Dabula, Anglican priest Harry Wiggett, who ministered to Mandela for three years while he was in Pollsmoor, and Mandela's grandson, Mandla Mandela.

Who then to believe? Mandela himself, or the many people who can testify to having witnessed his spiritual side, either while he was in prison or after he became president? It seems Mandela used to say one thing in public about his religious beliefs, and then something else entirely to individuals he encountered on a personal basis. In the same interview in which he denied being a spiritual person, he offered a possible reason for his public stance on religion in response to a question about his belief in God: "As I have said, the relationship between a person and God is personal. The question concerning the existence of God is something I reflect on in solitude."[4]

Mandela's answer makes it clear that he considered acts of worship and spiritual meditation to be private affairs. Those who engaged with Mandela on an individual level and were able to discuss religion with him confirm that he made a concerted effort to keep his religious beliefs to himself. Desmond Tutu corroborates this argument, adding that Mandela was "very, very private" about his spiritual life, even when he was given the opportunity to use religion to advance the political cause of the ANC.[5] Regardless of this, Mandela still acknowledged the relevance of religion in his own life, as well as its tremendous ability to bring people together and to mediate differences:

Yes, I certainly recognize the importance of the religious dimension of my own life. More important for me, however, is the significance of religion for countless numbers of people I meet both in South Africa and around the world. Religion is important because at the center of the great religious traditions is the pursuit of peace. South Africa needs peace, the world needs peace and I am convinced that if we were to put into practice the central tenets of Christianity, Judaism, African traditional religions, Buddhism, Hinduism, Islam and other faiths – all of which have a lot in common – there would be peace in the world ... I have no problem with religious belief. My problem is that all too often people fail to act on what they claim to believe.[6]

When Mandela said this, South Africa was undergoing a transition from apartheid to democracy, from a system of government that afforded human rights to only a privileged few, to one that would view all people as equals, regardless of race or creed. Mandela was going to be the leader of this new South Africa, and because he recognized the diversity of opinions and beliefs that made this country a "rainbow nation," he had to ensure that they all obtained an equal standing in the eyes of government and the Constitution. As the living representative of this law, the individual required to uphold it regardless of any constraints, Mandela therefore saw it as his duty to personally stand up for the beliefs of every person it was required to protect. This is why he chose to keep matters relating to his faith private, even if it had been crucial in alleviating many of his anxieties and fears during the long years of his incarceration, and through all the challenges of his presidency.

Christianity had been a vital component of Mandela's spiritual makeup long before his imprisonment on Robben Island. With his traditionalist father's approval, he had joined the Methodist Church in childhood. Gadla Mandela's hope was that his son's baptism into the religion of the white people who had claimed authority over his birthplace would present Mandela with opportunities from which many black people were excluded at the time, such as an education. Gadla's hopes were fulfilled when Mandela obtained a missionary education that also ended up shaping his political ideology. Mandela would later credit the schooling that he and many of his fellow political activists received at Methodist institutions with creating the kind of independent minds that had contributed to the anti-apartheid struggle.

But despite the significance he attached to the Christian religion in his own life, there was never any space in Mandela's worship of it to condemn or undermine other belief systems. In fact, Mandela's spirituality only strengthened his desire for reconciliation and forgiveness in a country that had almost been destroyed by prejudice and intolerance. During his presidency, and even while he was in prison, Mandela always found time to worship with different religions and Christian churches in his determination to promote acceptance among South Africa's various religious groups. The most remarkable product of Mandela's profound appreciation of Christian concepts, however, was the Truth and Reconciliation Commission (TRC), which he hoped would deal with crimes committed during apartheid without having to resort to Nuremberg-style trials for wrongdoers. Headed by Archbishop Desmond Tutu, the commission determined to confront many of the wrongs that were committed under white rule, but in the spirit of reconciliation and forgiveness.

Years before his death in 2013, Mandela had requested that his burial service observe traditional Methodist rites. With this final salute to the church that had cultivated his spirituality, Mandela had at last provided an answer to those who had always questioned his religious beliefs, or who had thought of him as an atheist or an enemy of the Christian faith. When his coffin was lowered into the ground, it was his friend, confidant and fellow Methodist, Bishop Don Dabula, who officiated over his burial, performing the traditional Methodist committal, in an act that illustrated the mutual love and regard that both church and follower had always held for each other.

1

Spiritual Origins

D URING NELSON MANDELA'S early childhood in Mvezo, a
village situated next to the Mbashe River in the Transkei,
he would often listen to tales told by his elders about the resistance
efforts the Xhosa had waged against the advance of Europeans in
their territory, and of chiefs such as Makana, the first Xhosa war-
rior to lead an attack against the British during the Xhosa Wars in
1819. Mandela was enthralled by accounts of Makana's courage
and brazenness, both of which led to the prophet's imprisonment
on Robben Island – the same prison where Mandela himself would
languish for nearly two decades.

But that date was written far in his future. At this point in his
life he was not a famous political icon, but a cattle-boy in his village,
known as Rolihlahla to his parents Gadla Henry Mphakanyiswa
Mandela, the chief of Mvezo, and Nonqaphi "Fanny" Nosekeni,
the third of Gadla's four wives.

Born on July 18, 1918, Rolihlahla was Gadla and Nosekeni's
first son, but the fourth and the youngest of all of his father's sons.
Gadla Mandela was a member of the Thembu tribe, from the
minor Ixhiba, or Left Hand House, where the king's counsellors
resided. Although he was not from the Great House – the house of
the kings – and would never be king himself, he was still possessed
of a royal heritage. His wife, Nosekeni, was also descended from

royalty, from the Thembu's Right Hand House, and her son with Gadla could therefore boast a royal ancestry that had been bequeathed to him by both his parents.

But even with the privileged position Gadla held among the Thembu people, there was no denying the tragic and inevitable fact that his world was changing. The arrival of British settlers in the Eastern Cape in 1819 and 1820 had brought with it the encroachment of Western laws and ideas on the Xhosa, as well as the displacement of traditional Xhosa beliefs with the Christian faith, which British Christian missionaries sought to entrench among some of South Africa's indigenous peoples. By the time Nelson Mandela was born in 1918, white authority had continued to excel in its efforts to undermine long-established Xhosa social structures.

The British government had indeed contrived to settle a large number of British immigrants in South Africa's Eastern Cape as a means of enforcing their rule in the area, so that the likes of Gadla Mandela, so-called Xhosa royalty, could be kept in their place. Britain's intention was for the settlers to form an English-speaking human fence in the area that would defend the Cape Colony from the fearsome Xhosa tribes that had already fought several frontier wars with European settlers – a plan that was not communicated to the immigrants before they arrived on the Cape's shores. In December 1819 and January 1820, when the 4,000 British settlers sailed across the Atlantic to the Cape, enthusiastic, optimistic and hopeful, they naively believed that they were leaving the unstable economic climate of their homeland to colonize a natural paradise that would make them wealthy and the masters of large, fruitful plots of land.[1]

The settlers were composed of individuals from a number of

Britain's social and economic classes. They included tradesmen, fishermen, sailors, manufacturers and artisans, as well as some farmers, most of whom were ill-equipped to handle the requirements of farming previously untouched land, and to defend the colony against dangerous Xhosa tribes. There were also settlers who were looking to do more than advance their economic prospects in Africa, such as those eager to spread the message of the Bible to the continent's indigenous inhabitants. The English missionary William Shaw belonged to this group.

Shaw came from a military family and, like his older brother – who was a sergeant in the same regiment – he was headed towards a commissioned rank in Britain's regular army. This all changed in December 1812, when Shaw, not yet fourteen, joined the society of Methodists at Colchester Barracks in Essex County. After embracing Christianity through Methodism, Shaw left his regiment in Ireland in July 1815, determined to become a foreign missionary. To this end, he applied for a job, but the news that he had been accepted never reached him because of postal delays. He decided to marry his fiancée instead, and since the Methodist Church did not accept probationary missionaries who were married, Shaw seemed to have destroyed any chance of becoming a missionary.

However, his hopes were raised once more when he heard that a group of tradesmen and their families, brought together by their Methodist beliefs, had formed a joint-stock party under the leadership of a carpenter from London and were planning on immigrating to South Africa. They needed a minister to accompany them, and Shaw got the job, sailing to South Africa in February 1820, and arriving in the country in May of the same year.

Shaw settled in the district of Albany, where he ministered to dejected and disgruntled settlers, as well as to British troops. Eventually, the members of his parish, which lay between the Bushman's and Fish Rivers, numbered 20,000, with an immigrant representation of 15,000, and the rest made up of soldiers, Dutch farmers and Khoi people.

Shaw clearly had a knack for missionary work, but something – a sense that he was needed somewhere else – had been tugging at his conscience for a long time. He soon came to believe that this nagging feeling had been placed in his heart by God as a sign that there was another group of souls – to be found among the Xhosa people – that needed to be converted to the Christian faith. Furthermore, these souls would have to be converted from their old customs and traditions in order to find salvation in the Christian religion and its saviour, Jesus Christ.

The idea was not new to Shaw. When he had first arrived in southern Africa, he had recognized the potential of its eastern coast as a "wide field" for establishing a string of mission stations beyond the colonial border, where scores of "unbelieving blacks" could be converted and ministered to.[2] Shaw would prove himself to be both uncompromising and single-minded in fulfilling this aim.

But inevitably, and in spite of Shaw's good intentions, the enforcement of Western beliefs and ideals on Xhosa culture met with a lot of resistance, for they experienced it as, in Noel Mostert's words, an "all-encompassing revolution against their ancestral past, the very fibre of their existence."[3] Many Xhosa people proved to be just as set in their religious and traditional beliefs as the Europeans who were trying to convert them. And in the latter's efforts to do so, there seemed to be no space for compromise on their part, mostly because they considered Xhosa culture to be barbaric and inferior to the supposedly civilized Christian faith.

The missionaries looked down on a number of Xhosa practices and beliefs, including the Xhosas' view that there was no such thing as an afterlife, and thus no reward or punishment for anyone after death – an idea that many Christians would find distressing or absurd. Instead, the Xhosas believed that their forefathers were ever present in their lives, and that they had to be kept content so that they did not inflict punishment or retribution on their living descendants. There were other Xhosa traditions – such as the nudity they frequently displayed, their belief in witchcraft and the circumcision of teenage boys – which the missionaries found abhorrent, but these were rituals that had been practiced and revered for centuries. While Europeans could find it easy enough to regard an uncircumcised adult Xhosa male as a man, among his own people he would be scorned for not having followed the traditional rite of circumcision to manhood. This same conflict of ideas applied to the practice of polygamy, an acceptable custom in Xhosa culture. But to any claim of cultural relativism, Shaw responded, "The custom of the country is nothing. The law of God is greater than any custom."[4]

This Christianizing onslaught against Xhosa culture could not go unchallenged. Xhosas who refused to accept or adopt European customs found ways of intimidating those who had converted to Christianity, such as forcibly seizing their cattle. Soon, however, the upheaval known as the Mfecane brought refugees fleeing from the Zulu king Shaka into the Eastern Cape, forcing Xhosa chiefs to reconsider the protection that could be offered to them by the colonial military power, and thereby providing missionaries with an opening for the harvesting of potential converts. Missionaries could communicate with colonial rulers while also offering education, which was seen by the Xhosa as a means of acquiring British skills and advantages. The Gqunukhwebe was the first Xhosa tribe to exploit these opportunities. Kama, the brother of the principal chief, the pragmatic Pato, was one of Shaw's most distinguished followers, although the missionary believed that Pato himself "greatly valued our mission, because it is a civil and political benefit to himself, but I fear he hates the Gospel."[5]

Nevertheless, the opposition to white rule and the missionary cause continued to escalate until a boiling point was reached with the cattle-killing disaster of 1856–57, when the Xhosa prophetess Nongqawuse predicted a resurrection of the Xhosas' power and the defeat of white authority if they collectively slaughtered all of their cattle and no longer cultivated their lands. If the prophecy was followed accordingly, Nongqawuse claimed, whites and the Xhosa refugees who had adopted their religion, along with all other unbelievers, would disappear into the sea, while those who obeyed the prophecy would experience a resurrection of their former power and wealth. The missionaries' warnings to Sarili, the paramount chief of the Xhosa, of the catastrophic effects that destroying their cattle would have on his people's livelihood went unheeded. Soon, vultures and other carrion eaters found themselves in a veritable paradise as rotting carcasses littered Xhosa territory, while starvation, poverty and the displacement of thousands followed for the Xhosa tribes. Many had to turn to the Cape Colony for relief from their suffering, with the knowledge that the killing of their cattle had had the opposite effect to the promised outcome.

The Xhosa, who had formed part of the migration of Bantu-speaking people from the Great Lakes region of subequatorial Africa around 2,000 years ago, had contributed to the displacement of the Khoi people following their settlement in the Eastern Cape. Now they had become a conquered people as well. Having always kept their kraals closed to the missionaries, they were now forced to open them, and Shaw, that pioneering missionary, was free to establish his mission stations throughout the Eastern Cape and to educate Xhosa people on Western beliefs and customs. However, the Xhosas' acceptance of the religion of their white conquerors notwithstanding, they would not be their equals in this new society.

When Shaw finally left South Africa in 1860, four decades after his arrival, he could rest easy in the knowledge that he had fulfilled his vision of establishing a trail of Methodist mission stations from the Eastern Cape into Natal. With his efforts, the Methodists were able to institute thirty-six mission stations stretching as far as Edendale in Natal, with an estimated 5,000 church members, ninety-six school teachers and forty-eight day schools. It is due to Shaw's determination to spread the Christian message to the Xhosa people that they now make up the biggest group of worshippers in the Methodist Church in South Africa.[6]

For Gadla Mandela, this encroachment of Western ideals on the traditional Xhosa way of life had revealed its malevolence in the way that white rule had been exercised in Mvezo since the British annexed it in 1885.[7] As a general rule, any opposition to British authority was judged not by laws with which the Thembu were familiar, but by foreign concepts, imposed with an iron hand.

In 1918, Gadla found out that it was better to adapt to these changing circumstances than to rebel and face humiliation. Shortly after his son Rolihlahla's birth, he was called before the colonial magistrate following a complaint lodged against him by one of his subjects. Gadla, who questioned the magistrate's authority and stood by the principle that the customs of the Thembus, and not those of the king of England, should apply to him, refused to appear in court. He was a man steeped in custom, and a believer in Qamata, the god worshipped by his forefathers. He also occupied an important position in his village as an informal priest, which allowed him to direct rites for harvesting and the slaughtering of goats and calves, and to officiate at birth, marriage, initiation and funeral ceremonies. To the colonial magistrate, however, he was merely a subject of white rule, and his insolence was punished with a charge of insubordination and the removal of his chieftainship. Gadla's wealth, which came mostly from cattle and land, was also significantly reduced, and, no longer a chief but a peasant in the eyes of the law, he was unable to care for his family as he once did. Nosekeni moved with her baby to Qunu – the village that would become famously linked with her son's name, and where the course of his life would be altered forever.[8]

For the dispirited Gadla, the episode with the magistrate served as a valuable lesson, and he began to reflect on what the future held for his family and his people. He eventually came to the realization that life would be far better for individuals who possessed a Western education, as it would be the educated among the Xhosa who would be able to understand the ways of white people, speak their language, and thus be able to adapt to their world. However, such an education was a privilege provided only to those who attended school, and in the Transkei region it was the Methodist Church alone that ran schools for Xhosa people. If Gadla's fourth son was to amount to anything, he would have to attend a church school.

Gadla's belief that a church education would bring his son prosperity was based on his observations of the Mfengu, a tribe formed from the groups of people that had fled to the Eastern Cape during the Mfecane of the early nineteenth century. The Mfengu refugees had been among the first to work for whites, and even sided with them in the Frontier Wars, an act for which they were disliked by the rest of the Xhosa, who considered them traitors. They were also the first converts to Christianity, turning their backs on their old, traditional beliefs, and preferring to wear Western clothes and to reap the benefits of European culture. Many of them were educated and worked as policemen, clerks, teachers, interpreters and in the clergy. They were also generally more affluent than the rest of the Xhosa community, and were among the first to build houses and to utilize modern farming methods. The success they enjoyed, as well as their alliance with whites, engendered a large amount of animosity against them among the Xhosa people. But to the likes of the pragmatic Gadla, who could no doubt spot the link between their adoption of the white man's religion and their prosperity, the Mfengu, according to his son, "confirmed the missionaries' axiom, that to be Christian was to be civilized and to be civilized was to be Christian."[9]

Gadla was evidently a man who could look beyond the jealousies and petty resentments which the rest of the Xhosa harbored against the Mfengu, and he chose instead to obtain the same privileges for his son. While both he and Nosekeni were illiterate, Gadla recognized that being able to read and write would enable Rolihlahla to pursue the kind of career that was usually only the preserve of children of the Mfengu. He also saw the importance of religion in accomplishing this goal, and while he never converted to Christianity himself, he had allowed Nosekeni to join the Methodist Church, a decision that was unusual for the kind of patriarchal society in which they lived. Gadla soon permitted his youngest son's baptism into the church as well.

Gadla counted as his friends the Mbekela brothers, George and Ben, who were both educated Methodists. To the brothers, there was something appealing about the young Mandela, something that stood out as they watched him play or herd sheep, or whenever they had a conversation with him. Their intuition about his potential moved them to act, and George Mbekela, who was a school teacher, had a discussion with Nosekeni in which he told her, "Your son is a clever young fellow. He should go to school."[10]

This was a pivotal moment for both the Mandela family and for South Africa, as Nosekeni's decision of whether or not to send her son to school would determine which path his life would follow: whether he would grow up to remain in Qunu and carve out a life for himself there as the son of a former chief, or whether he would go to school and learn a trade, stepping out into the wider world of the Eastern Cape, and perhaps the rest of South Africa. Nosekeni decided to bring the matter to Gadla, who, faced with an opening to give his son the kind of future that he had long wished for, immediately realized that Rolihlahla should go to school.[11]

The school Rolihlahla would attend was situated in Qunu and run by Methodists, whose missionaries Gadla's grandfather, the great King Ngubengcuka – known as the father of the Thembus – had invited into his kingdom in the early nineteenth century. The kingdom, which included Mthatha and Queenstown, and which was occupied by peoples such as the Hlubi, Tshangase and Bhele, had been under threat owing to continual wars between its tribes and to its many conflicts with Europeans. To prevent any further division between the peoples in his territory, the king decided to allow the missionaries to preach their faith to his people, which he hoped would unite the warring tribes with one another and with the Europeans in the area through a shared respect for a new god and religion.[12]

King Ngubengcuka never adopted Methodism himself, but it seems his descendant, the perceptive Gadla, had inherited his pragmatism. With the assistance and advice of the Mbekela brothers, the young Rolihlahla Mandela was to embark on a new life that would remove him from the rural and traditional one he knew as a member of his father's household and educate him in the ways and beliefs of the Wesleyans. He would become the first member of the Mandela family to attend school, these first steps into a Methodist education determining the path he would eventually take to his unlikely destiny as president of South Africa.

2

A Methodist Education

IN 1925, ON the day before seven-year-old Rolihlahla Mandela was due to start school, his father, Gadla, took him aside and told him that he had to be properly dressed for the occasion. Until that moment, the boy had only ever worn a blanket wrapped around one shoulder and pinned at the waist.

Rolihlahla's parents could not afford to buy a new school uniform for him. Instead, he watched as his father took a pair of his old trousers and cut them at the knees. When he tried the pants on, the length suited him fine, but they were too wide for him, so Gadla used a piece of string to tighten them at the waist. "I must have been a comical sight," Mandela said, reflecting on the occasion decades later, "but I have never owned a suit I was prouder to wear than my father's cut-off pants."[1]

The next day at his school, where all lessons took place in a single room, the boy's introduction to a Methodist education was marked by his teacher, Miss Mdingane, giving him and the rest of her students a Christian first name. For the remainder of his time at school, Rolihlahla would be called Nelson, a name he would go on to wear for the rest of his life. His mother, who had been christened "Fanny" when she became a Christian, pronounced her son's new name as "Nelisile."[2] "This [acquiring of an English name] was the custom among Africans in those days and was undoubtedly due to the British bias of our education," said Mandela. "The education I received was a British education, in which British ideas, British culture, and British institutions, were automatically assumed to be superior. There was no such thing as African culture."[3] This emphasis on British values and superiority would underscore Mandela's entire Methodist education, and greatly influence his way of thinking and how he perceived the world.

When he was nine years old, Mandela was in his mother's hut when his father, who had an undiagnosed lung disease, suffered through the last moments of his life. Throughout his illness, he had been taken care of by Nosekeni and his youngest wife, Nodayimani. Now they were forced to watch as Gadla smoked his pipe for one last hour before quietly slipping away.

Before he died, Gadla – who had known that he did not have long to live – had ensured that his youngest son was suitably provided for. He sought help from the acting paramount chief of the Thembu people, Jongintaba Dalindyebo, who had become regent largely due to Gadla's intervention, and the two men came up with a plan for Mandela's future. Imploring the regent, Gadla had said: "Sir, I leave my orphan to you to educate. I can see he is progressing and aims high. Teach him and he will respect you." And Jongintaba, mindful of the fact that he owed Gadla a debt, had promised, "I will take Rolihlahla and educate him."[4] With the attainment of this oath, Gadla would have been able to die with the knowledge that he had done everything in his power to give his son a better chance at a successful life. His appeal to the regent said much of his love for the boy.

Following his death, Gadla received a Christian burial, even though he had never converted to Christianity in his lifetime. The ceremony was the idea of the Methodist Mbekela brothers, the young Mandela's early mentors, and revealed just how much influence they had over the Mandela family. In accordance with traditional rites, a cow was also slaughtered and Gadla was laid to rest in the local cemetery. For the young Nelson Mandela, who had greatly looked up to his father, the death marked a change in how he came to see himself. "I do not remember experiencing great grief so much as feeling cut adrift. Although my mother was the center of my existence, I defined myself through my father. My father's passing changed my whole life in a way that I did not suspect at the time."[5] One of these changes required Mandela to move away from Qunu to live in the provincial capital of Thembuland, Mqhekezweni, or the Great Place, the home of Jongintaba and his family.

Mandela would have to leave his mother and set out for his new home following a period of mourning for Gadla. The loss of his father was thus not what distressed him the most during this time. "I mourned less for my father than for the world I was leaving behind," he noted. "Qunu was all that I knew, and I loved it in the unconditional way that a child loves his first home. Before we disappeared behind the hills, I turned and looked for what I imagined was the last time at my village."[6]

Nosekeni and her son shared a deep bond, and she, too, must have been greatly saddened about having to part with him, especially so soon after losing her husband. But the regent was not the kind of man whose offer of help could be refused, and in his promise to be a guardian to Mandela, Gadla had secured a great opportunity for his child. Mandela would be brought up in a Christian home and attend school, while still being educated on the traditions and rites of the Thembu by one of the tribe's great leaders. This was a privilege that Nosekeni could not deny Mandela, and, spiritual as she was, she would have known that her son was in good hands.

On the morning that Mandela was to go and live with Jongintaba, he and Nosekeni set out for the Great Place. They walked for hours, throughout the morning and into the early afternoon, mother and son, up and down hills and on dirty roads, each step taking them further away from Qunu and closer to Mandela's new home and life. Few words passed between them, "But the silence of the heart between mother and child is not a lonely one," observed Mandela. "My mother and I never talked very much, but we did not need to. I never doubted her love or questioned her support."[7]

When the Great Place was finally within their sight, it was like something from a dream to Mandela: "a vision of wealth and order beyond my imagination," he remembered. He watched in awe as a Ford V8 drove up to the residence and the men guarding the gates stood up to acknowledge the authority of the driver with the traditional Xhosa salutation for their chiefs, *Bayethe a-a-a, Jongintaba!*"

When Jongintaba, whose name means "one who looks at the mountains," got out of his car, Mandela was struck by his appearance. "He was a man with a sturdy presence toward whom all eyes gazed. He had a dark complexion and an intelligent face, and he casually shook hands with each of the men beneath the tree, men, who I later discovered, comprised the highest Thembu Court of Justice. This was the regent who was to become my guardian and benefactor for the next decade."[8]

The shy boy, carrying a tin trunk and clothed in a khaki shirt and old khaki shorts held up by a belt made of string, was entranced by the scene, which was unlike any he had witnessed in humble

Qunu. For the first time, Mandela, who had never been able to see his father lead a tribe, could observe the power and authority of a chief, and he felt something deep inside him respond to it:

> Until then I had had no thoughts of anything but my own pleasures, no higher ambition than to eat well and become a champion stick-fighter. I had no thought of money, or class or fame, or power. Suddenly a new world opened before me. Children from poor homes often find themselves beguiled by a host of new temptations when suddenly confronted by great wealth. I was no exception. I felt many of my established beliefs and loyalties begin to ebb away. The slender foundation built by my parents began to shake. In that instant, I saw life might hold more for me than being a champion stick-fighter.[9]

When Nosekeni left Mandela with Jongintaba a few days later, a change had already set in for the boy, symbolized by the replacement of his well-worn clothes with a handsome new outfit purchased for him by his guardian. His parting with his mother seemed to lack any emotion, Nosekeni offering no words of wisdom to her son or giving him any goodbye hugs or kisses. "I suspect she did not want me to feel bereft at her departure and was matter-of-fact," Mandela said. "I knew that my father had wanted me to be educated and prepared for a wide world, and I could not do that at Qunu. Her tender look was all the affection and support I needed."[10]

However, just as Nosekeni left to return to her own world – her son's former home – she betrayed some of the emotion she must have been feeling when she suddenly turned to Mandela and said: "*Uqinisufoktho Kwedini*" (Brace yourself, boy).[11] Mandela, excited about what was waiting for him in the Great Place, would find all the motivation he needed in Nosekeni's parting words to face the unknown future that lay ahead of him.

At the Great Place, Mandela made friends with the regent's two children – Justice, Jongintaba's only son and heir, and Jongintaba's daughter, Nomafu. Four years older than the introverted Mandela, Justice was tall, handsome and outgoing, and was popular with girls. He became Mandela's new hero after the loss of Gadla, and would play a mentoring role in the impressionable boy's life.

Mandela's first school in Mqhekezweni was next door to the palace. His teachers, Mr. Fadana and, later, Mr. Giqwa, both took a keen interest in the newcomer, who excelled at his lessons through perseverance rather than any particular brilliance.

Jongintaba in the meantime was working on a plan that would ensure that Gadla Mandela's son lived up to his full potential. Jongintaba was adamant that Mandela would not become a migrant worker who would in adulthood join the annual exodus of hundreds of young men from Transkei to Johannesburg to work underground in South Africa's gold mines. Nor was he going to become another one of the millions of illiterate black South Africans who were reduced to working as cheap labor in a white-run economy. "It is not for you to spend your life mining the white man's gold, never knowing how to write your name," Jongintaba told his charge as often as he could.[12]

To Jongintaba's mind, Mandela's destiny was to become a royal counsellor, and there was no place where he could better prepare for this role than the Great Place. There was also no one more equipped or with better authority to guide him towards this destiny than the regent himself, who knew much about culture and religion, the two principles that would govern Mandela's education at the Great Place. In this world where Mandela would have to enforce traditional justice as a royal counsellor while still assimilating the tenets of Christianity – which espoused as their primary values forgiveness and loving your neighbor as yourself – religion and tradition occupied equally important roles, although their relationship with each other could be rather fraught. In order to carry out his duties as both a Methodist and a member of the Thembu tribe, the young Mandela would therefore have to learn how to accord the required amount of respect and devotion to each of these forces in his life without neglecting one in favor of the other.

Before moving to the Great Place, Mandela had only been to church once, when he had been baptized at the Methodist church in Qunu. In his father's home, he had indulged in religion merely for his mother's sake, and had thought of it as simply a ritual.[13] At the Great Place, however, the church and Christianity played a central role in family life. Jongintaba and his wife, No-England, who treated Mandela as if he were her own child, were serious about their family regularly attending the mission church, a legacy of William Shaw's work in the area in the early nineteenth century. On church days, men would dress in suits, and women, complying with the missionary-favored dress code, wore long skirts and high-necked blouses, scarves around their necks and blankets draped over their shoulders.[14]

The young Nelson Mandela was expected to join the family in church every Sunday without fail, and it was here, in the figure of the mission church's leader, Reverend Matyolo, that he began to witness the power of another, very different type of authority from what he had encountered before. A stout man in his mid-fifties, with a resonant voice that regularly preached fire and brimstone in his sermons, Matyolo was as popular and beloved in Mqhekezweni as the regent. In the reverend's view, God was wise, omnipotent and vengeful, and did not let bad deeds go unpunished – ideas which made a powerful impression on the young Mandela. "For me," Mandela said, "Christianity was not so much a system of beliefs as it was the powerful creed of a single man: Reverend Matyolo. For me, his powerful presence embodied all that was alluring in Christianity…. But the Church was as concerned with this world as the next: I saw that virtually all of the achievements of Africans seemed to have come about through the missionary work of the Church."[15]

But even with this awareness of the reverend's authority, Mandela still found the courage to steal some maize from his garden, which he then roasted on the spot. Unfortunately, someone witnessed the deed and reported him to the minister. At prayer time that evening, a daily ritual in the Dalindyebo residence, No-England chastized Mandela for stealing from a servant of God and shaming the family.[16] It seems that Mandela was pushing and crossing boundaries even as a boy.

In 1934, when Mandela was sixteen years old, he was compelled to participate in another ritual: the traditional Xhosa rite of circumcision. Jongintaba might have headed a Christian household, but there were some traditions that had to be followed if a Xhosa male was to be respected and thought of as wise among the Thembu – and, above all, if he was to be considered a man. Without undertaking this passage from boyhood, no uncircumcised Xhosa male could become his father's heir, or marry or officiate at tribal rituals.

"For the Xhosa people," Mandela said of this momentous occasion in his life, "circumcision represents the formal incorporation of males into society. It is not just a surgical procedure, but a lengthy and elaborate ritual in preparation for manhood. As a Xhosa, I count my years as a man from the date of my circumcision."[17]

In spite of the devout Christian beliefs held by Jongintaba and many other Xhosa people in Thembuland, circumcision still endured as a powerful means of conveying a boy's journey to manhood.

There were twenty-six boys in Mandela's circumcision school, which was situated in a valley on the banks of the Mbashe River. Their circumcision was performed by a respected *ingcibi*, or circumcision expert, who used his assegai to remove the foreskin during the procedure. Mandela watched as the *ingcibi* carried out the first circumcision. The boy shouted out afterwards, "*Ndiyindoda!*" (I am a man!), the traditional cry of initiates following their circumcision. It was Justice's turn next. Of his own experience before the *ingcibi*, Mandela remembered:

> There were now two boys before the ingcibi reached me, and my mind must have gone blank because before I knew it, the old man was kneeling in front of me. I looked directly into his eyes. He was pale, and though the day was cold, his face was shining with perspiration. Without a word, he took my foreskin, pulled it forward, and then, in a single motion, brought down his assegai. I felt as if fire was shooting through my veins; the pain was so intense that I buried my chin in my chest. Many seconds seemed to pass before I remembered the cry, and then I recovered and called out "Ndiyindoda."[18]

Mandela was growing into a man of wisdom, undergoing the traditional but painful rite of circumcision while also learning to become a devout Christian through his regular attendance of church and his schooling.

In the same year that he was circumcised, Mandela began high school at Clarkebury, which was situated in the district of Engcobo, the core of a Methodist network of forty-two outstation schools in Thembuland. Clarkebury had a good reputation and was home to a teacher's college and a training institute for tradesmen such as carpenters, shoemakers and printers. For the Thembu people, the Clarkebury mission station held a particular significance because it stood as a reminder of Mandela's great-grandfather, King Ngubengcuka, who had promised William Shaw land on which to start a mission station. That land became Clarkebury, founded in 1825 by Reverend Richard Hadley and named after the British theologian, Dr. Adam Clarke.[19]

Jongintaba, a Clarkebury Old Boy like his son Justice, drove Mandela to the school on his first day in his Ford V8, but not before he had slaughtered a sheep to celebrate the boy's promotion from Standard Five to high school. This was the first party that was thrown in honor of Mandela's achievements. He also received his first pair of boots from the regent, which, despite being brand new, he proudly polished to wear on his first day at school.

During the drive, Jongintaba spoke to Mandela about responsibility, honor and reverence for the family name, just as a father speaks to his son before a significant event in the latter's life. Jongintaba urged his young charge to behave in a manner that brought respect to him as well as to his brother, future king Sabata Dalindyebo, and Mandela assured Jongintaba that he would not let him down. During the conversation, Jongintaba also explained what Mandela's future role in Thembu society would be, and since this would be brought about by Jongintaba's tutelage, Mandela could be assured of his importance among the Thembu people. The regent explained that when Sabata was older, he would also be put in the care of the Clarkebury headmaster, Reverend Cecil Harris, whom Jongintaba admiringly described as a white Thembu. Reverend Harris would help train Sabata to become a Christian and traditional leader, so it was crucial that Mandela make the best of his education at Clarkebury under the reverend's guidance. "He said I must learn from Reverend Harris because I was destined to guide the leader that Reverend Harris was to mold," Mandela recalled.[20]

When they arrived at Clarkebury, Jongintaba led Mandela – who at this point in his life had had very few interactions with white people – to Reverend Harris, who shook his hand. It was the first time that he had been greeted in such a way by a white man. Mandela was told that he would receive no special or preferential treatment at the school, although he might have assumed that his connection with King Ngubengcuka, who had played such a pivotal role in the spread of Methodism in Clarkebury, would give him some leverage there.

Mandela spent three years at Clarkebury before transferring, when he was nineteen years old, to another prestigious Methodist institution, the Wesleyan college of Healdtown. Established in Fort Beaufort in 1855, Healdtown was even more impressive than Clarkebury, boasting more than 4,000 male and female students and offering a Christian and liberal arts education based on the English model. Colonial buildings covered in ivy emphasized that this was a place where the African elite was being educated to become "black Englishmen as we were sometimes derisively called. We were taught – and believed – that the best ideas were English ideas, the best government was English government, and the best men were Englishmen," Mandela said of the learning environment at the school.[21]

Sunday was the day of the week when the influence of British imperialism was on full display at Healdtown: boys and girls, dressed in white shirts, black blazers and maroon and gold ties, would march to the church, where the Union Jack was raised and the school brass band played as the students sang "God Save the King" and "Nkosi Sikelel' iAfrika."[22] Yet it was at this same breeding ground where young black people were taught to assimilate the ideals of a foreign civilization that Mandela found himself parting with the rather parochial view of life he had held until then, and the wider idea of his African identity began to assert itself. His Xhosa identity continued to maintain a profound place in his mind as well, and he would go on to see himself as being proudly Xhosa first and African second.

In his final year at Healdtown, in 1939, Xhosa poet and *imbongi* (praise-singer) Krune Mqhayi paid a visit to the school – an occasion that further fueled Mandela's interest in his native culture. The *imbongi*'s songs, which predicted that black Africans would one day rise up against the interlopers in their land and achieve their freedom, touched and stirred the Xhosa heart beating in Mandela's breast: "Now, come you, O House of Xhosa, I give unto you the most important and transcendent star, the Morning Star, for you are a proud and powerful people. It is the star for counting the years – the years of manhood," Mqhayi chanted. These words rooted themselves firmly in Mandela's mind and helped to feed the freedom fighter within him for many years to come.[23]

At Healdtown, Mandela also witnessed another first when Reverend Seth Mokitimi, the house master of his dormitory, stood up to a white man's attempts to intimidate him.

Dr. Arthur Wellington, the stuffy English principal at Healdtown who ruled imperiously over the school and habitually bullied his staff, had decided to intervene one night during a dispute between two prefects over which Reverend Mokitimi was mediating. Mokitimi had been handling the affair very capably before Dr. Wellington arrived at the scene, behaving, Mandela recalled, "as if God had descended to solve our humble problem."[24]

A group of boys, which included among their number Nelson Mandela – by this time long accustomed to seeing white people abuse their power over black people – watched keenly as Dr. Wellington demanded to know of Reverend Mokitimi what was going on between the two boys.

If they had been expecting Mokitimi to cower before his taller, white boss, they were mistaken. Speaking calmly and respectfully, Mokitimi assured Dr. Wellington that the situation was under control and that he would give the principal a rundown of events the next day. When Dr. Wellington insisted that he wanted to know what the issue was right then and there, Mokitimi maintained his earlier stance: "Dr. Wellington, I am the housemaster and I have told you that I will report to you tomorrow, and that is what I will do."

The boys in the dormitory, including Mandela, were stunned. "We had never seen anyone, much less a black man, stand up to Dr. Wellington, and we waited for an explosion," Mandela said.[25]

But the blow-up never came. Dr. Wellington simply said, "Very well," and exited the dormitory.

The incident left a lasting impression on Mandela, as would the courageous figure of Reverend Mokitimi, who would go on to become the first black president of the Methodist Church in South Africa in 1963. In standing up to his white superior, the reverend had in an instant transformed the way that Mandela perceived black and white relations. No longer would he acknowledge Dr. Wellington as the god which the principal had previously portrayed himself to be, nor would the Reverend Mokitimi be regarded as a mere lackey. To prove his worth in society, a black man did not have to automatically defer to white people, no matter how highly ranked they were.

It was the second time in his life that Mandela had seen the influence that men of the cloth could exercise over others, having witnessed it before as a boy during Reverend Matyolo's church services. And it was just the beginning of his contact with the quiet power and authority that religious leaders commanded.

3

The Runaway

IN 1939, THE year Europe went to war, twenty-one-year-old Nelson Mandela arrived at the University College of Fort Hare as one of a group of 150 black students.

These students formed part of the elite in a world where black people were lucky to learn how to read and write, never mind receive a tertiary education. And yet even the potential success of this fortunate group of students would be tempered by the inequalities of the time, given that their university education would typically only take them as far as the civil service. Groomed as Mandela was for success, the most he could probably hope to do at this stage in his life, even with a university degree, was to work as a clerk or an interpreter at the Native Affairs Department.

Fort Hare had been a church-driven project, its governing council comprised of representatives from the Anglican, Methodist and Presbyterian churches. Situated under the Amatola Mountains on the banks of the Tyhume River, it was built on land donated by the United Free Church of Scotland and opened in 1916.[1] By the time Mandela attended the college, it had established a reputation as an institution promoting strong Christian values among its students. Mandela actively participated in this religious environment, joining the Student Christian Association and teaching Bible classes on Sundays in the villages surrounding Fort Hare.[2] The kinds of minds that were cultivated at the university at this time can be seen in the number of freedom fighters who form part of its alumni, including, in addition to Nelson Mandela, Oliver Tambo, Robert Mugabe, Seretse Khama, Dennis Brutus, Govan Mbeki and Robert Sobukwe.

The principal of the college, Dr. Alexander Kerr, was passionate about the English language, and he stoked in Mandela's mind an appreciation of English poetry. Decades after he had left Fort Hare, Mandela could still recite verses from poems that had inspired him during his studies at the college. One of his favorites was Alfred Lord Tennyson's "In Memoriam A.H.H.":

> Strong Son of God, immortal Love
> Whom we, that have not seen thy face,
> By faith, and faith alone, embrace,
> Believing where we cannot prove....[3]

Later in his life, Mandela expressed his gratitude to missionaries for furthering the knowledge of black Africans through the educational institutions they had established in the Eastern Cape: "Our generation was produced by Christian schools, by missionary schools … when the government took no interest whatsoever in our education. It was the missionary that piloted black education.... So Christianity is really in our blood."[4]

Fort Hare, in particular, greatly influenced the social, intellectual and political development of the young Mandela, whose interactions in the worldly atmosphere of the university were far removed from the kinds he had experienced in rural Qunu. "Fort Hare's worldliness may not seem much, but to a country boy like myself, it was a revelation," he said.[5] During his time at Fort Hare, Mandela met and socialized with black individuals from other parts of South Africa and from further afield, and such encounters made an impact on the way he thought about the world. In this way, he was given the opportunity to assimilate ideas and engage in conversations or debates that were not limited by a purely religious or cultural rhetoric. It was also at the university that he was introduced to the kind of lifestyle that those living outside of rural areas generally took for granted. At Fort Hare, Mandela wore pajamas for the first time, persevering in sleeping in them every night, even though he found them initially uncomfortable. He also swapped the ash he had been using to brush his teeth for toothpaste, and replaced the blue detergent with which he usually washed himself with soap.

There were a number of extracurricular activities he took up as well, such as boxing and ballroom dancing, the mastery of which was considered an accomplishment by the aspiring young elite at Fort Hare. The dining hall became his training ground, where he would practice the foxtrot and the waltz in an attempt to emulate the moves of world ballroom-dancing champion Victor Silvester.[6]

On one evening, Mandela's love for dance nearly got him into a lot of trouble when he decided, in the hope of trying out his moves on an actual dance floor, to visit a dance hall that was usually out of bounds for undergraduates, although popular with the educated elite. Full of bravado, he requested a dance from a young woman, who, while in his arms, revealed that her name was Mrs. Bokwe. Mandela was horrified. Mrs. Bokwe was the wife of the respected and highly esteemed Dr. Roseberry Bokwe, the brother-in-law of one of Mandela's professors, Z.K. Matthews, who just happened to be in charge of university discipline. As soon as he could, Mandela apologized to Mrs. Bokwe and stole off. He had broken a number of university regulations, but, to his relief, Professor Matthews never mentioned anything of the indiscretion to him.

This was just one of the many new and exciting exploits that were made available to the young man from Qunu by his university education. He would go on to join the Dramatic Society, learn how to box, and train in cross-country racing, an activity that impressed on him how a combination of dedicated exercise, discipline and diligence could count for more than natural ability. It was a value that he would apply to his work for the rest of his life. Many of the activities in which Mandela participated at Fort Hare were fun, too, and, having looked at things from a rather serious point of view before then – his nickname in the Great Place was *tatomkhulu*, or "Grandpa", because of his somber bearing – he learned to take things less seriously and to start enjoying his youth.

At Fort Hare, Mandela found a new mentor in his nephew, Kaiser Matanzima, who was three years older than him and a third-year student. The two men had initially bonded over their familial connection, but soon the tall and confident Matanzima became one of Mandela's closest friends, sharing a number of interests with his younger relative in spite of the latter's lack of worldly experience. Methodism was one of the things that united them, and they regularly attended church together. Matanzima eventually arranged for Mandela to move into the Methodist residence in which he stayed at Fort Hare: Wesley House, a two-story building with room for sixteen beds. He also shared his allowance with Mandela, and introduced him to football. Matanzima would go on to become the first Xhosa chief to obtain a university degree, which indicates how ambitious and serious he was – traits that probably appealed to the impressionable young Mandela. The two were inseparable at Fort Hare, as Matanzima would later fondly recall: "When someone saw me alone, they would ask 'Where's Nelson?' ... We had warm hearts together."[7]

The university was also the place where Mandela forged his first political connections, some of which would endure even during the turbulent years of the struggle against apartheid. One of these was Oliver Tambo, who, like Mandela, would go on to lead the ANC. At Fort Hare, Tambo became a close friend of Mandela and Matanzima, although he resided at the college's Anglican hostel, Beda Hall, which was regarded as the most imposing residence on campus. Tambo was a more somber man than Mandela, but as a fellow Sunday-school teacher and member of the Student Christian Association, he shared Mandela's commitment to promoting the Christian faith among the Eastern Cape's youth. In fact, Tambo was such a devout Christian that he considered becoming an Anglican minister before his political obligations got in the way of this ambition.[8] Tambo and Mandela are examples of the kind of free-thinking and revolutionary individuals that religious schools and universities helped to mold in a period of South African history when most black people struggled to receive a proper education.

Mandela's friendship with Tambo would grow stronger through the years, "into an enduring partnership that found firm expression in politics, law and life," according to Tambo. But the same could not be said of their relationship with Matanzima, who came to be viewed by both men as a traitor to the anti-apartheid struggle following the support he gave to the Bantu Authorities Act of 1951, when he was chief of the "emigrant Thembus," a subgroup of the Thembu tribe. The Act, which the apartheid government claimed would bring about the self-determination of South African tribes through the creation of a federation of black states, naturally undermined the goal of freedom for black South Africans which Mandela, Tambo and the rest of the ANC were advancing. Tambo was particularly disdainful of Matanzima's choice, claiming that "Kaizer Matanzima was to become a political disaster for the victims of what became known as apartheid, and was a great gift to the strategists for the permanent European domination in South Africa. His contribution to the consolidation and survival of apartheid was to prove greater than any other black man."[9] That his erstwhile mentor and role model became a major supporter of the National Party's dream of separate development, essentially stripping him and millions of other black people of their South African citizenship, disappointed and hurt Mandela.

During his time at Fort Hare, and even while he became more of a sophisticate, Mandela never lost sight of the fact that the love and sacrifices of others were what had allowed him to obtain the opportunities that had been made available to him. He might have been raised by the regent and his wife in the comfort of the Great Place, but a large portion of Mandela's loyalty and affection still belonged to his mother. She had always been the spiritual beacon in Mandela's life, the person whose Christian counsel, as described by writer and political activist Fatima Meer, was embedded in his "consciousness in spite of other ideological strains that enter it."[10] Indeed, Nosekeni's devotion to the Christian faith was an anchor of stability in what would be an otherwise turbulent existence for Mandela, and it helped to remind him of who had fed his spiritual beliefs and had brought about his education at Methodist institutions. He felt a deep gratitude to her for the role she had played in the formation of his religious identity, and, because of this and everything else she had done for him, he never lost the desire to improve her life and to make up for what she had lost when Gadla's chiefdom was taken away. In his second year at Fort Hare, in 1940, he therefore attacked his studies with renewed vigor, his eyes fixed on October when he would write his finals and be rewarded with a university degree – his passport to financial success and to restoring Nosekeni's wealth and prestige. "I would build her a proper home in Qunu, with a garden and modern furniture and fittings," Mandela remembered thinking at the time. "I would support her and my sisters so that they could afford the things that they had so long been denied. This was my dream and it seemed within reach."[11]

But Mandela's upward mobility in student politics would defer this dream. When students at Fort Hare called for a boycott of elections for the Students' Representative Council (SRC) to express their dissatisfaction with the quality of the food being served to them, Mandela, a candidate in the election, gave his support to the boycott. Some students still went ahead and voted, and Mandela was elected. However, he and the five other elected SRC members resigned as they allegedly did not enjoy the support of the majority. They were outmaneuvered, however, when Fort Hare called for new elections and they found themselves re-elected. Mandela, who could not accept this result, resigned, but his five co-members did not – a decision which prompted Dr. Alexander Kerr to threaten Mandela with expulsion if he would not withdraw his resignation. Mandela agonized over what to do, but he eventually took Matanzima's counsel to not change his mind, and told Dr. Kerr the next day that he would not compromise on his decision to leave the SRC. Dr. Kerr advised that he think over this decision during the summer holidays and return to university the following year only if he was prepared to be on the SRC.

When Mandela returned to the Great Place to inform Jongin-taba of what had happened, he found an unsympathetic ear in his mentor, who instructed Mandela to return to Fort Hare in autumn. No further discussions would be brooked by the regent.

However, it was not Mandela's resistance to serving on the SRC that would take him away from Fort Hare, but rather Jongintaba's plans for his future. The regent had been ill for some time, and fearing that he would not be alive for much longer, he had made arrangements, without Mandela's or Justice's knowledge, for them to marry two women from the Thembu tribe. What is more, the woman Jongintaba had found for Mandela was actually in a rela-tionship with Justice, who was in love with her. Mandela had no feelings for his fiancée at all, so he attempted to wiggle out of the engagement, approaching No-England, whom he referred to as the Queen, with an offer to return to Fort Hare, where he would complete his studies and only then find another woman, approved of by the regent, to marry. No-England agreed with the plan, but Jongintaba would not entertain the idea and insisted that Mandela go through with the marriage he had already arranged for him.

The regent, however, no longer had the same hold over Mandela that he had possessed before. Schools such as Clarkebury and Fort Hare had exposed Mandela to different kinds of people with dif-ferent ideas and cultures from his own, and he was not the same naive boy who had been so awestruck by the regent's power when he had first arrived at the Great Place. His education, albeit under the watchful and at times severe scrutiny of institutions that ad-vanced religious dogma, had helped to make him an independent thinker who could decide for himself what was good for him. And marrying a woman who his friend was in love with, and with whom he was not, ultimately went against what he believed to be right. He chose not to submit to the regent's demands, valuing his loyalty to Justice above his ties to tradition, and he decided to leave the Great Place. Justice chose to do the same.

The decision naturally grieved Mandela, who, in running away from the Great Place to Johannesburg, would effectively be terminating Jongintaba's guardianship over him. He was not only openly defying the conventions of his people, but he had even gone so far as to convince the regent's son to do so, too. The rebel in Mandela, rather than the royal counsellor, had finally revealed himself. For the rest of his life after making this choice, Mandela would continue to value personal freedom above any system of belief that required blind submission from its followers. This aspect of his character would show itself most evidently in his political career and the commitment he showed to his future political party, the ANC.

4

Politics, Before Anything Else

I T WAS AT a place where the regent swore Nelson Mandela would never work that the young man found his first job in Johannesburg after moving to the city in 1941. Crown Mines, the biggest gold mine in Johannesburg, had lured thousands of migrants from rural areas throughout South Africa to work underground as cheap, exploited labor – and now it seemed that Jongintaba's adopted son had also been taken in by the mines' false promises.

Mandela, however, did not work underground during his time at Crown Mines. The former university student, who had herded animals as a boy in Qunu, was a night watchman at the company, standing guard at the compound's entrance to ensure that only those who were authorized could enter. It was a job that would have been unworthy for someone of Mandela's status back in Thembuland, a man who had been raised to counsel Xhosa leaders.

Justice, the son of the Thembu regent, also worked at Crown Mines as a security guard. He and Mandela had found their jobs through the mine's chief *induna* or headman, Piliso, who had to be convinced by the two young men that the regent approved of them working there – the first of many lies they would tell when they initially arrived in Johannesburg. Mandela and Justice twisted their story in a way that made it at least half true, using the fact that Jongintaba had previously written to Piliso to arrange for Justice to get a clerical job in Johannesburg as their reason for needing work in the city now. When Piliso voiced his doubt about this, Justice assured him, with another lie, that a letter from the regent explaining Mandela's presence was on its way. Eventually, after plying Piliso with falsehoods, Mandela and Justice persuaded him to help them. They were soon caught out, however, when they were heard boasting about their trickery to one of the men who worked underground. The truth reached Piliso who, incensed, castigated them before ordering them to leave the mine.[1] Mandela and Justice were humiliated, as well as destitute, as they had no place to stay and no job prospects.

They eventually found refuge in the home of Mandela's cousin, Garlick Mbekeni, who performed an even bigger act of kindness when he introduced Mandela to a man he described as "one of our best people in Johannesburg."[2] This man's name was Walter Sisulu, and he, along with Oliver Tambo, would join Mandela's ranks as one of South Africa's foremost freedom fighters. By the time he met Mandela, Sisulu had already distinguished himself in Johannesburg as an estate agent, prominent businessman and local leader. He was also the illegitimate son of a white magistrate, Albert Dickenson, who later became a judge at the Johannesburg Supreme Court.[3]

An urbane and confident young man, Sisulu was proficient in English, and was able to give Mandela the impression that he was a university graduate. He only grew in Mandela's estimation when Mandela learned later that Sisulu had not advanced past Standard Six at school. The success Sisulu enjoyed, despite his lack of education, would alter Mandela's belief that having a Bachelor of Arts degree was one of the hallmarks of a leader. Having witnessed so many kinds of leaders in the period before he moved to Johannesburg –

in Jongintaba's household, at school and at church – Mandela had been under the impression that having an education was the only way he could become a leader himself. However, through Walter Sisulu's example, Mandela learned, again, that ideas, no matter how entrenched, could be questioned and even overturned.

Mandela also impressed Sisulu. His dignified bearing, royal connections and ambition made Sisulu realize that he was, in his own words, in the presence of "a bright young man with high ideals."[4]

Sisulu listened as Mandela, leaving out his reasons for absconding from the Great Place, spoke of why he had not completed his education at Fort Hare and about his plans to be a lawyer, which he would achieve by studying for a degree through the University of South Africa (UNISA) via correspondence. He hoped that studying law would provide him with the skills to fight for justice for black South Africans. It was clear by now that the fire the missionary schools had ignited in Mandela to become a useful member of society was burning more intensely in Johannesburg.

Sisulu promised Mandela that he would speak to a white lawyer, Lazer Sidelsky – whose firm, Witkin, Sidelsky and Eidelman, was one of the biggest in Johannesburg – about career opportunities for his new friend. Sidelsky was able to find a position for Mandela at his firm as a clerk, for which Mandela would earn two pounds a month. The young Jewish lawyer proved to be a good employer when, in 1942, after Mandela had completed his BA degree and was articled, he upped his salary to eight pounds a month. The pay was the same as that received by black factory workers, but for Mandela it was nonetheless a huge sum of money. In later years, Mandela would remember Sidelsky as "the first white man to treat me as a human being." In fact, Sidelsky would become very much

47

like an older brother to Mandela, giving him one of his old suits and a shirt to wear to work, as well as a loan of fifty pounds to help him buy food and other essentials when he first began working at the law firm.[5] Such acts of kindness from men like Sidelsky, who at the time were not obligated or expected to assist black people in any way, helped to shape Mandela's view – one that would survive even when he was an old man in prison – that good could be found in any kind of person, from any racial background or faith. Mandela's natural ability to draw in many types of people with his charm also worked on Sidelsky, who remembered him as being "conscientious, never dubious, tidy in person and in mind."[6]

In helping to get Mandela settled in Johannesburg, Sisulu had disobeyed an instruction given to him by the then president of the ANC, Dr. A.B. Xuma, a migrant from the Transkei and an old friend of Jongintaba, who had explained to Sisulu why Mandela and Justice had fled to Johannesburg. Because of the disobedience they had displayed towards the regent, Xuma urged Sisulu not to help Justice or Mandela in their pursuits in Johannesburg. However, despite the rift that had formed between Jongintaba and Mandela, reconciliation between the two men would take place in 1941 when the ailing regent, while visiting Johannesburg, sent a message to his former ward inviting him to come and see him. It was not a request that could be refused, even if Mandela was nervous about coming face to face with the man who had raised him as a son, and whom he had betrayed when he had left his house. However, when he finally encountered his former guardian, he found a somewhat mellowed old man who did not mention Fort Hare or the arranged marriage. "He was courteous and solicitous, questioning me in a fatherly way about my studies and future plans," Mandela said.

"He recognized that my life was starting in earnest and would take a different course from the one he had envisaged and planned for me. He did not try and dissuade me from my course, and I was grateful for this implicit acknowledgement that he was no longer in charge."[7]

Jongintaba had raised Mandela in a strict Christian household, and in his ability to forgive his adopted son, he proved himself to be a good and devout Christian who prized forgiveness and reconciliation – traits which Mandela would adopt in later life in his dealings with apartheid injustices. For Mandela, this was an important meeting, as it freed him from the guilt he had been feeling for so long about leaving his home, and helped to restore his regard for the Thembu royal house. It also allowed him to continue pursuing a new path in life. "I had become indifferent to my old connections, an attitude I had adopted in part to justify my flight and somehow alleviate the pain of my separation from a world I loved and valued. It was reassuring to be back in the Regent's warm embrace," Mandela later confessed about the encounter.[8]

Jongintaba had reconciled with Mandela, but he still hoped that Justice would return with him to the Transkei to take up his royal duties. Mandela, however, was unable to persuade Justice to leave Johannesburg. Neither Justice nor Mandela would see Jongintaba alive again, as the regent died six months after his Johannesburg visit.

In the same year, 1941, Mandela moved to the overcrowded, squalid slum of Alexandra, which seemed to have no shortage of *shebeens* or gangsters. Residents of the township referred to it as Dark City because it had no electricity. But to Mandela, it was his own version of heaven, an urban Promised Land where life constantly hung in the balance even while opportunities were never far away. It was in Alexandra where Mandela found his first home away from his old life and, as a result, the township always held a special place in his heart.[9]

His address was 46 Eighth Avenue, where he lodged with a fellow Thembu and family friend, Reverend J. Mabutho, a minister in the Anglican Church. Mandela chose to withhold his reasons for leaving the Transkei when he went to live with the reverend. As many of his elders would have thought his conduct dishonorable, Mandela found it easier to omit certain facts in his account of why he was in Johannesburg. Also, confessing what he had done to a religious leader was an intimidating prospect, and he would have been worried about being viewed as unreliable and a liar by a representative of the Christian church. He was nevertheless caught out in his lie when a visitor to the house recognized him and mentioned the Crown Mines affair. The next day, Reverend Mabutho asked Mandela to leave his house. However, fervent Christian that he was, the reverend did not entirely abandon Mandela, arranging for him to move into a room in 46 Seventh Avenue with the Xhoma family. Situated at the back of the property, the sparse room with its dirt floor and tin roof had been built by the Xhomas merely as a means of earning an extra income, and it contained no conveniences such as running water or electricity.

At night, Mandela had to study by candlelight and he seldom had anything to eat but a mouthful of food or the bread or occasional meal the secretaries at his work shared with him. Sundays were his favorite day, as he was allowed to join the Xhoma family for lunch and eat his only hot meal of the week. Food, studies and rent used up all of his wages, and he hardly had any money for clothes. For the next five years he would wear Mr. Sidelsky's suit to work, and it was not uncommon for him to go without a change of clothing. He also had to walk to work in the morning and home at night on most days. And yet, even while suffering through all of these discomforts, Mandela was happy, because for the first time in his life he had his own place to call home. Christian schools such as Clarkebury and Healdtown might have helped him become acquainted with comforts like beds and pajamas, but living in the harsh, impoverished environment of Alexandra required him to recall the hardships of his childhood before he attended missionary schools, when he had nothing to call his own.

Mandela also found time for romance during this period. He was somewhat awkward and hesitant around women, but when he fell in love with a Swazi woman, Ellen Nkabinde, a friend from his Healdtown days, most of this shyness melted away. They spent whatever free time they had together, often walking in the surrounding veld and hills near Alexandra. Reverend Mabutho's wife, however, was averse to Mandela seeing non-Xhosa women and actively tried to break up their relationship, which ended anyway when Ellen, who had always given Mandela a lot of support and guidance, moved away. Soon after Ellen, Didi, one of the five Xhoma daughters, began to attract his attention, but she had given her heart to her wealthier boyfriend who drove a car and was a far better catch than the poor Mandela.

In spite of all of these romantic complications, Mandela was never distracted from his studies, and in 1942 he passed his final examination for his BA, which distinguished him as the first Mandela with a degree. He was still determined to become a lawyer and, the following year, enrolled as a part-time student at the University of the Witwatersrand's law faculty, where he was the only African student. It was while he was studying law, in 1944, that he met Evelyn Mase, a beautiful young nurse, at Walter and Albertina Sisulu's house in Orlando, Soweto.

Evelyn was smitten with Mandela from the moment she met him. "I think I loved him the first time I saw him," she said. "The Sisulus had many friends. They were such genial, generous people and Walter had lots of friends who came to their home, but there was something special about Nelson."[10]

Mandela was swept off his feet by the quiet twenty-two-year-old from Engcobo. He flirted with her in the Sisulus' living room, and joked that he would visit her at the Non-European General Hospital in Hillbrow, Johannesburg, where she worked. True to his word, Mandela later appeared at the hospital to see her.

Soon they were engaged to be married. However, the couple could not afford a traditional wedding or feast, so they settled on a civil ceremony at the Native Commissioner's Court in Johannesburg as opposed to a church wedding. Both Evelyn, who was a Jehovah's Witness, and Mandela would probably have been upset by this. Mandela would also have been disappointed that he could not afford to have his beloved mother attend the wedding and that it would not be a traditional Xhosa affair, which she would have appreciated. He did not pay *lobola* (a bride price) for Evelyn either. The move to Johannesburg had required many sacrifices, including those related to tradition and religion, yet it had given Mandela independence, too. He was now free to marry whomever he chose, regardless of any constraints. Walter and Albertina Sisulu were the couple's witnesses at their wedding.

The Mandelas had very little money and lived in poverty, something that became a contentious issue in their relationship. A lack of money meant that Mandela could not take Evelyn to Qunu to meet Nosekeni. The couple, like many other black people at the time, also had to deal with the country's housing shortage and struggled to find accommodation, living at first with Evelyn's brother in Orlando East, then with her sister. In 1946, they moved with their one-year-old son, Madiba Thembekile ("Thembi"), into a two-roomed municipal house in Orlando East, and later took possession of a bigger house in Orlando West. Residents mockingly referred to the area as Westcliff, the name of an affluent neighboring area for whites, but there was nothing grand about Orlando West, and the kind of houses built for the residents of the township – the hundreds of identical, tin-roofed units situated on dwarf-like plots with no electricity or toilets, all running along untarred roads – reflected what the white government really thought of them. Nevertheless, Mandela was proud of the home he had found for his family. "It was the very opposite of grand, but it was my first true home of my own and I was mightily proud. A man is not a man until he has a house of his own. I did not know then that it would be the only residence that would be entirely mine for many, many years," Mandela said later in his autobiography.[11]

But witnessing such poverty on a daily basis, and experiencing it himself, affected Mandela's perceptions of black society. Studying the Bible at school and church meant that he was well aware of the Christian concept that all people were created equally in the eyes of God. Yet this idea did not underpin the law of the supposedly Christian government of the National Party. Mandela just had to step outside his house in Orlando West and take a look at how he and the rest of South Africa's black population were living to come to terms with the kind of inequality that had produced such living standards. Christianity also promoted learning and schooling among black South Africans, but the white government made a determined effort to keep them uneducated – an effort that would be realized in the Bantu Education Act of 1953, which enforced the creation of segregated education facilities for black people and basically put an end to the missionary schooling from which they had previously benefitted. The poverty that Mandela witnessed every day, as well as the desire his Methodist education had instilled in him to continue to better himself, helped to keep alive his ambitions to complete his university degree and become a lawyer.

In 1947, the Mandelas' second child, Makaziwe, was born. She was a frail baby who required constant nursing, and her parents feared for her health. When she was nine months old, she became ill and died a few days later. "We were heart-broken," Evelyn said of the loss.[12] The death of the baby devastated the Mandela household. Evelyn was distraught, as was Mandela, but he hid his grief so he could give his wife his full support.[13] This ability to depend on his own, inner strength would become a permanent aspect of Mandela's character, one that he would put to good use throughout the struggle and during the many years he spent in prison. He could always find the motivation to focus on decisions and actions that would prevent despondency and inspire him to move forward. The birth of his and Evelyn's second son, Makgatho, in 1950, probably also contributed to soothing his grief somewhat.

Also in 1947, Mandela completed his articles at Witkin, Sidelsky and Eidelman, and resolved to become a full-time student in the hope that he could one day open his own legal practice. But this meant he had to quit the firm, which lost him his salary of eight pounds. He took out a loan of 150 pounds, but the financial strain on the family was immense and a constant source of tension in his marriage.

During this time, Mandela became increasingly involved in politics. In 1948 he was elected national secretary of the ANC Youth League (ANCYL), his first official position in the organization, much to Evelyn's consternation. She was unhappy with how much time he spent away from home on ANC business. Thembi had even asked her at one point, "Where does Daddy live?"[14]

After 1948, a marked change in the politics of the ANC occurred as the party replaced previous resistance policies of moderation, such as deputations and petitions, with more militant displays of mass mobilization. Some of the activities defining this aspect of the resistance struggle were boycotts and strikes, which found ultimate expression in the Defiance Campaign of 1952. The campaign sought to carry out acts of civil disobedience on a national scale and through non-violent means, which included protesters deliberately breaking apartheid laws they considered unjust or against their civil liberties, and openly inviting arrest. Prior to the launch of the campaign, the ANC and the South African Indian Congress (SAIC) had called on protesters to observe April 6, 1952, the day on which white Afrikaners celebrated the tercentenary of Jan van Riebeeck's arrival at the Cape, as "A National Day of Pledge and Prayer."[15] The "prayer" aspect of the protest unequivocally helped to underline the fact that the God invoked by the apartheid government was also the God of the oppressed.

The Defiance Campaign was officially launched on June 26, 1952. Mandela, who by this time had been named president of the

Transvaal branch of the ANC, was made the Defiance Campaign's volunteer-in-chief who would lead the non-violent protests against apartheid laws. The first stage of the campaign maintained this stance of non-aggression, but by November of that year, violence had erupted in areas such as Johannesburg, Kimberley and East London.[16] In the last area, crowds of rioters protesting white oppression engaged in a number of violent acts, including burning down institutions they associated with European rule, such as churches and mission stations. Anglican and Roman Catholic churches, as well as a Catholic mission station, were set on fire by the rioters, with the only thing remaining of the last building "a charred crucifix at the entrance to the school."[17]

Albert Luthuli, who was one of the leaders of the Defiance Campaign and who would soon become ANC president, was saddened by the destruction of such places of worship. However, he was not blind to the feelings that motivated the rioters as they targeted these buildings, saying of the damage that was done to the churches:

> When a church is burned down, some whites say, "But a *church* – I simply cannot understand it." Others say, "There, you see! They even burn down churches because they are barbarians!" But how far is it not tragically true that these churches have become distorted symbols? How far do they stand for an ethic which the whites have brought, preached, and refused to practice? "You close your eyes obediently to pray," goes the saying, and "when you open them the whites have taken your land and interfered with your women."
>
> How far do these churches represent something alien from the spirit of Christ, a sort of patronizing social service?[18]

With these words, Luthuli highlighted the hypocrisy with which
the apartheid state used religion and the church to subjugate the
black masses, the justification being that Christianity was the preserve of the white race, since all other races were either too barbaric
or unworthy to be true believers. Luthuli went further by explaining
the pointlessness of such a racialized notion of Christianity, given
that the faith's aim has always been to unify its followers in a single
system of belief and fellowship.

> White paternalist Christianity – as though the whites had in-
> vented the Christian Faith – estranges my people from Christ.
> Hypocrisy, double standards, and the identification of white
> skins with Christianity, do the same. For myself, for very many
> of us, nothing short of apostasy would budge us. We know
> Christianity for what it is, we know it is not a white preserve,
> we know that many whites – and Africans for that matter – are
> inferior exponents of what they profess. The faith of Christ
> persists in spite of them.[19]

In his call for "apostasy" of the belief system that helped to sustain
ideas of racial inequality in South Africa, Luthuli drew attention to
the way in which the ANC's political focus was evolving, as first
indicated in the shift from more restrained acts of resistance to
those carried out in the Defiance Campaign. No longer would the
ANC allow the white government to dictate to them what was right
or wrong in the furthering of their cause against racial injustice and
segregation. This was the start of the party's journey from peaceful
protest to the armed struggle – to the idea that the continued inflic-
tion of a hypocritical apartheid ideology on the minds and spirits

of black people would have to be met with force. Mandela, who since moving from the sheltered traditional environment of the Great Place had rapidly assimilated political ideas calling for the autonomy and liberty of black Africans, and then of all South Africans, would fully embrace the idea of an armed struggle.

On July 30, 1952, at the height of the Defiance Campaign, Mandela had been part of a group of protesters who were arrested by police. He was charged under the Suppression of Communism Act, and in December of that year he was banned for six months from attending any meetings and leaving Johannesburg, and from talking to more than one person at a time.

The banning order essentially turned Mandela into a prisoner, restricting his movements and cutting him off from the politics that had become his lifeblood. He also experienced first-hand the painful psychological effects of the isolation that this kind of punishment engenders. "Banning not only confines one physically, it imprisons one's spirit," he said. "It induces a kind of psychological claustrophobia that makes one yearn not only for freedom of movement but spiritual escape.... The insidious effects of bans was that at a certain point one began to think that the oppressor was not without but within."[20] Luthuli also underlined this capacity of the apartheid state to infiltrate areas of everyday existence, such as religion, in order to impose its ideology on the minds of those over whom it exercised power. A complete oppression of the spirit of the individual was the result of giving in to this form of brainwashing, and was a fate that those who suffered under apartheid had to battle against constantly in order to retain the belief that they were not inferior to the people who were telling them otherwise. Mandela would have to fight such ideas each time he was persecuted by the state in his struggle for freedom.

In an effort to counteract some of the negative effects of his banning order, he began to work on a plan that would allow banned ANC members to continue to interact with other members of the party without having to meet in public. Such a strategy would also be useful in the event of the ANC becoming a banned party, which was beginning to look like a real possibility.[21] The plan became known as the M-plan, or the Mandela plan, and it required that the ANC be broken down into cells in order to keep operating underground even if it was declared illegal, taking as its example the procedures that the Methodist Church employed for its church-building and recruitment initiatives. Mandela himself, however, admitted that the M-plan only had a modest success rate in the ANC and was not widely adopted.[22] Even so, it is telling that he turned to the church that had helped to nurture his political and spiritual growth during the unhappy period of his banning order, when he longed for "spiritual escape" and the means to continue participating in the struggle.

As miserable as Mandela was in his virtual exile, his neglected wife, usually so starved of his company, welcomed his confinement to their home.[23] By now, Evelyn, despite being married to a man she loved, was suffering from a deep loneliness, and she greatly resented the politics and the political group that were keeping her husband away from her. Perhaps in an attempt to find friends or to detach herself from her troubled home life, she had developed an intense devotion to her Jehovah's Witness church, which had begun to drive a wedge between her and Mandela. This religious fervor had intensified soon after Makaziwe's death, and Evelyn, in her desperation for another daughter, had fallen into the habit of praying for another child. When she eventually became pregnant and gave birth to a girl, also named Makaziwe, in 1954, Evelyn viewed this as a sign from God. "It was then that I began my return to my Christian faith," she said.[24]

Thereafter, Evelyn dedicated her life entirely to the Jehovah's Witnesses, a decision that caused her to clash regularly with her husband over their very different beliefs. At one point she made the almost unforgivable mistake of telling Mandela that her religious faith served a higher purpose than his political ambitions, and she tried to get him to join her church. The couple would draw their children into their squabbles as well, Evelyn taking them to church whenever she could, reading the church's *Watchtower* magazine to them, and having them distribute church literature in their neighborhood. Mandela's response was to teach them about politics and to not speak to his wife.[25] The kind of Christianity with which he had grown up, and which he had come to admire, had not been about complete submission to authority. Instead, it was a form of empowerment, the only means for many black South Africans to obtain an education or a career other than that of menial labor. He therefore could not and would not share the kind of devotion to religion that Evelyn possessed. "There was an obsessional element to it that put me off," he remarked about Evelyn's religious beliefs. "From what I could discern, her faith taught passivity and submissiveness in the face of oppression, something I could not accept. My devotion to the ANC and the struggle was unremitting. This disturbed Evelyn. She always assumed that politics was a youthful diversion, that I would someday return to the Transkei and practice there as a lawyer."[26]

Mandela and Evelyn's unyielding positions made a separation inevitable, and Mandela seriously began to consider divorce. "A man and a woman who hold such different views of their respective roles in life cannot remain close," he said. "We were finding no common ground and I was convinced that the marriage was no longer tenable."[27]

But the ANC had not been the only focus of Mandela's attention during his marriage to Evelyn. In 1952 he had joined up with his friend from Fort Hare and the ANC, Oliver Tambo, to start a law firm in Johannesburg, which they named Mandela and Tambo. Although Mandela did not complete his LLB at Wits, he had received a two-year diploma in law, which, along with his BA degree, allowed him to practice as a lawyer – a career that he loved.[28] Mandela relished the moments he spent in the courtroom, where he was allowed to freely engage with white people in defense of his clients without any fear of being punished. His court appearances soon became legendary among Johannesburg's black residents, who found Mandela's exchanges with whites – devoid of the simpering or deference that was usually required from black people in these situations – liberating. He also gained a reputation as a sophisticated and suave man because of the smart suits he wore and the fact that he drove his own car, which was unusual for a black man during this period in South Africa's history. Mandela was clearly very different from the majority of men in his community, and people began to treat him as such, especially women. All of these factors naturally began to affect his behavior as well, and, for a while, politics and the temptations that power and visibility had brought him detracted from his devotion to his wife, contributing to the weakening of their relationship.

Mandela and Evelyn had been living apart since 1952 while she did a course in midwifery in Durban, and by 1953 rumors began to circulate about his infidelity with Lillian Ngoyi from the ANC Women's League. These rumors eventually reached Evelyn: "I could not place my finger on it at first. Nobody would tell me. Then the gossip reached me. Nelson, I was told, was having an affair with a woman member of the ANC. I knew this woman and admired and liked her. She visited us often and I got on well with her. I did not believe the rumor at first, but unable to bear it, I turned to Nelson. Who else could I have turned to? He was angry that I questioned his fidelity."[29]

In a desperate attempt to rescue her marriage, Evelyn went to Sisulu for help, but this only angered Mandela. She then solicited the help of Kaiser Matanzima, who broke the sad news to her that Mandela no longer loved her. Hurt and angry, Evelyn had an explosive argument with her husband before moving out of their house to live with her brother. Mandela persuaded her to forget the incident and to return home, which she did, but by then too much had happened, and they both knew that their marriage was over. "That chilling, unbearable distance continued. I realized that I had no marriage," she reflected. She moved out of their house again to her nurse's quarters in the hope that her husband would come to his senses and work harder to keep his family together. But Mandela neither messaged nor visited Evelyn at the nurses' home.[30]

By 1955, Evelyn had given Mandela an ultimatum that he decide with whom his loyalties lay – with her or with the ANC. But she had already reached her own decision about their marriage. On December 5, 1956, Mandela and 155 other political leaders were arrested in a raid and charged with treason. When he returned home shortly before Christmas, an empty house welcomed him: Evelyn had left with their children and taken everything, even the curtains – a detail that Mandela found "shattering." He was left with a mere shell of a home, devoid of love or the sounds of children playing and laughing.[31]

Mandela was now free to devote his time entirely to the anti-apartheid struggle. But this had come at a cost. Not only had he compromised certain aspects of his moral character to reach this point in his life, but he had also lost his family as a result.

5

Taking Up Arms

Estranged from Evelyn, though not legally divorced, Mandela was free to live his life the way he desired, and he began to dedicate nearly all of his time to politics and the ANC. By the time he had found a new companion in the young and beautiful social worker, Winnie Madikizela, there were no other forces demanding his attention or loyalty, and he had given himself over completely to his political activism. Any woman who entered Mandela's life during this period would have to accept the fact that his duty to the ANC came before any other aspect of his life.

Mandela wanted to marry Winnie from the moment he met her, and the connection they shared upon first seeing each other only strengthened when they learned how much they had in common. Like Mandela, Winnie had grown up in the Transkei, was descended from royalty and had been raised as a Methodist. She further impressed Mandela with her "spirit, her passion, her youth, her courage, her wilfulness," the kinds of traits befitting the partner of a political activist.[1] However, before they made any vows to each other, Mandela – whose first marriage had failed partly because of money issues – made it clear to Winnie that they would experience many hard times during their relationship. By this time, 1957, Mandela was still a defendant in the Treason Trial, which took up nearly all of his time and had caused his business to suffer as a result. If Winnie were to marry him, she had to accept that her small salary would probably have to support their entire family, and that her husband would sometimes be away from home for long stretches of time. "Winnie understood and said she was prepared to take the risk and throw in her lot with me," Mandela recalled. "I never promised her gold and diamonds, and I was never able to give them to her."[2]

Mandela went the traditional route in marrying Winnie, first by asking the Madikizela family for their approval of the union, which differed from how his marriage to Evelyn had been arranged. Indeed, his struggle to obtain custody of his children after he had failed to pay *lobola* for his ex-wife had probably helped Mandela to realize that there was no escape from tradition in his world, especially if the woman he chose to marry was a traditionalist. While moving to Johannesburg and joining the ANC had led him to attribute prominence to politics above all else, Mandela still had to find ways of assimilating the older, more arcane structures of Xhosa tradition into his personal life. He had grown up constantly toeing the line between tradition and religion, and he would have to do the same with tradition and his everyday existence. He also hoped to gain more support for the ANC from members of the African community, and showing greater regard for his cultural roots would help him to achieve this.

The Madikizela family, like the Mandelas, had been able to integrate Christian beliefs into their traditional way of life, too. Winnie's grandfather, Chief Mazingi, had struck up a similar deal to the one Gadla's grandfather, King Ngubengcuka, had made with the Methodists in the nineteenth century, by inviting them to settle in his own Great Place, Komkhulu. The far-seeing Mazingi had recognized that he was living in changing times and decided to accept the missionaries' God, in the hope that his descendants would be taught at missionary schools the same skills that had brought so many white people prosperity. In this way he was also like Mandela's father, Gadla, who had not been blind to the benefits that could be accrued by those who practiced the religious beliefs of the missionaries.

Mazingi's senior wife, Seyina, did not initially adopt her husband's Christian beliefs, but she ultimately learned to merge them with her own traditional values. The eldest of their six sons, Columbus Kokani, was a devout Christian who had grown up in a world where tradition was not perceived with the same reverence as it had been among older generations, and when it came to taking up the chieftainship, he chose instead to become a teacher like his wife, Nomathamsanqa Gertrude. Columbus's mother disliked his choice of spouse, not only because she was educated and a Christian, but because she came from a mixed family background, indicated in the blue color of her eyes. "Makhulu held my mother responsible for inhibiting her son, my father, from becoming a chief and a real man by taking more wives," Winnie has said of her family. "When he had announced his intention to marry her, she told him he was out of his mind, that he was marrying a 'European' not a Muntu, and a man and not a woman. 'Marry a wife,' she had advised, 'not a fellow teacher.' But having made her point she held her peace with her son, and blamed the woman for the *takhati* [witchcraft] she had put on him."[3]

As a girl, Winnie was frequently caught in the middle of the conflict that raged between her Methodist mother and traditionalist grandmother, each of whom tried to make her the depository of their individual belief systems. Nevertheless, Winnie's parents raised their daughter in a devout Methodist home, baptizing her in the Christian faith in 1936, the year she was born, and ensuring that she and the rest of their family attended church every Sunday, and that the children attended Sunday school. As it had in Jongintaba's household, Christianity took on a significant role in the Madikizela family. It was seen as an instrument that could bring about both spiritual enlightenment and a Western education. At the same time, Christianity also had to function side by side with the rules and rituals of Xhosa culture. But as relations between Winnie's mother and grandmother proved, this was not always easy to achieve.

In 1958, the year Winnie and Mandela wanted to marry, he was still banned and had to ask Winnie to travel to the Transkei without him to inform her parents of their plans. Winnie's parents were hesitant about their daughter marrying a man who was facing charges of treason and who would probably end up in prison at some point during their marriage. While Mandela had demonstrated that he wanted to spend the rest of his life with Winnie, the love of his life, the reality was that his devotion to the ANC meant he was essentially already married to politics. His first marriage had disintegrated for this reason, and Winnie's parents were worried that she was still too young to be able to cope with the pressures of being the wife of a political activist. Winnie, however, was in love and determined to have Nelson Mandela as her husband, and her parents soon realized that they could not stop her from pursuing this course in her life.[4]

Mandela's commitment to the struggle would indeed exact a number of sacrifices from both him and Winnie. Their marriage would not be a conventional one, tested as it was in the arena of resistance politics that would take up nearly all of Mandela's time, and eventually his freedom. To survive the future that was waiting for them, they would each have to rely on their own inner strength and the love that they had for each other, and to remember that any suffering they had to endure was for the benefit of a higher purpose.

Mandela's childhood friend, Justice, who was now Chief Justice Mtirara, along with another chief, Wonga Mbetheni, represented Mandela in the *lobola* negotiations for his marriage to Winnie. When the payment was made, Thembu chiefs brought the Mandela cattle to join the Madikizela cattle in one *kraal*, and the occasion was commemorated with the traditional feasting together of the two families. Back in Johannesburg, Winnie celebrated her engagement with Mandela, who was now officially her fiancé.

As Mandela could not leave Johannesburg, he had to ask for permission from a magistrate to attend his marriage ceremony, obtaining six days' leave of absence for the event. He and Winnie were married on June 14, 1958 at the Suduke Methodist mission station, twenty miles from the Madikizela homestead. Columbus led Winnie, wearing a white wedding dress, into the church, where she and Mandela were declared husband and wife by a Methodist reverend. Traditional rites also had a place in the ceremony, with an *imbongi*, dressed in tribal skins, paying tribute to both the Mandela and Madikizela lineages. Members of the ANC, the other great love of Mandela's life, were present, as well as a number of communists from the SACP, the political ideology of which Mandela had at first despised, although he grew to admire their stance of non-racialism and their contribution to the freedom struggle.

Mandela and Winnie's wedding seemed to symbolize the enormous change that had come over the political activist since he had first arrived in Johannesburg as a young university dropout. He was no longer the boy who had been forced to run away from the destiny that had been handed down to him by tradition and older men. There was also no need for him to constantly explain his motives, as he had done in his first marriage, because he had found the support of a wife who shared his political philosophy and understood the sacrifices that he would have to make to fight for his cause. Mandela could now dedicate his life to the liberation struggle, and he would not rest until he helped to obtain the freedom of the segregated peoples of South Africa. And while he never forgot the religious and cultural teachings he had received in his youth, these would, at this point in his life, have to take a back seat to the political goals and ideals that would help him defeat apartheid.

By the second half of 1958, the Mandelas had settled comfortably into married life. Nosekeni and Mandela's sister Leaby were living with them, and Leaby took the bus to work with Winnie every morning.[5] A month after their wedding, Winnie and Mandela were also expecting a baby. Mandela still stood accused in the Treason Trial, and he would usually have to take a bus to Pretoria every morning to attend court sessions. He and Winnie were very active in the struggle at this time, despite the constraints that had been placed on him by the trial and his banning order.

On February 5, 1959, Winnie gave birth to their daughter, Zenani. Arrangements were made for Zenani's baptism, which Alice Manse Sisulu, the mother of Walter Sisulu, hoped would be a traditional Xhosa one. Winnie, however, would not have Zenani placed in a traditional herbal bath for the baptism, as she considered this unsanitary.

Five months after Zenani's birth, the Mandelas' financial affairs improved slightly when Winnie found a job with the Johannesburg Child Welfare Society as a social worker. She also became pregnant with a second child, which she miscarried, but she was pregnant again within months.

At this time, the ANC was experiencing major conflict within its ranks, between members who disapproved of the role that white communists and Indians played in the party and who proposed a more militant stance against the white regime, and members who believed that South Africa belonged to all who lived in it, regardless of race. The conflict resulted in a schism between the two factions and the birth of a new party in resistance politics, the Pan African-ist Congress (PAC), which was made up of those former ANC affiliates who supported the aggressive reclamation of South Africa for black Africans before anyone else. With Robert Sobukwe, who had also attended Fort Hare, as its founding president, the party commenced activities on April 6, 1959.

The ANC soon found itself fighting a turf battle with its new rivals, who were determined to gain a powerful footing in the anti-apartheid struggle and to portray the ANC as sell-outs of the cause. On March 21, 1960, Sobukwe led the PAC in what it described as a march to "African freedom and the United States of Africa." As a non-violent demonstration against the pass laws, protesters refused to carry their passes and demanded their own arrests as a result. It was a daring and bold move by the PAC, but it resulted in the fatal shooting of nearly seventy demonstrators by policemen outside the Sharpeville police station. Nearly all of the victims, including the 180 injured, had been shot in the back as they fled. News of the Sharpeville massacre caught the attention of the rest of the world, and the United Nations Security Council condemned the act, blaming the South African government for a blatant abuse of power. The government responded by banning the ANC and the PAC.

Through Sharpeville, the fledgling PAC had changed the rules of the resistance movement, forcing the ANC to reassess their own tactics, many of which seemed to be ineffective in countering further abuses of justice by the apartheid government or in getting their message across. It was clear that a different form of protest was needed to reinvigorate the anti-apartheid struggle in the country; one that would allow the ANC to continue carrying out its initiatives as a banned party.[6]

While the party continued to search for solutions to this problem, Mandela left Johannesburg for Pietermaritzburg in March 1961 to attend the All-in African Conference, a meeting of 145 political organizations from all over the country to discuss the creation of a national constitutional convention for South Africa.[7]

Before he left, he returned home to say a painful goodbye to Winnie and his family. Mandela knew that his wife had the courage and strength of character to take care of their family by herself. She had given birth to their second daughter, Zindziswa, the previous December and now had two children to look after, but Mandela reassured her that she would get help from his friends in Johannesburg while he was away. However, he withheld from her just how long he would be gone and how dangerous his journey would be. He had served nearly all of his time on his banning order (something that Winnie was unaware of), but he believed that he would still be arrested if he was caught leaving Johannesburg. He also knew that regardless of how well the conference went, or whether he was arrested on his journey or not, he would not be returning home. He was ultimately placing the liberation struggle above his marriage and family.[8] Winnie, heartbroken and worried about her husband's departure, packed a suitcase for him, but did not ask him any questions about his plans, knowing that she would not receive any answers. "I only wished him well and asked that the gods of Africa take care of him wherever he should be, and that he would have a chance to spare the children and me a few minutes sometime." Mandela, however, "scolded me for reminding him of his duties."[9] Sensitive about the fact that he was leaving his family behind in Johannesburg to carry out his political duties, Mandela was probably not open to being reminded at that time of the responsibilities he had to his wife and children. His confidence in himself as the patriarch of his family seemed to convince him that he was doing the right thing in putting his country first.

In Natal, on March 25 and 26, 1961, Mandela addressed a panel of 1,400 delegates at the All-in African Conference, the first time in five years that he was free to speak from a public platform. He called for a convention in which South Africans of every race could come together to write a constitution that encompassed all of their aspirations, and threatened the South African government with a three-day national strike if the conference's demands were not met.

A National Action Council (NAC) was formed to implement the resolutions of the conference, and Mandela was appointed the leader of the council. Because of this, and even though, on March 29, he and the rest of the accused in the Treason Trial had been declared not guilty of conspiring against the government, Mandela knew that he would soon be facing legal trouble again and decided to go into hiding.

Life as a fugitive did not stop Mandela from fully engaging in the struggle, and he continued to forge new connections with individuals and groups who supported the liberation movement, including religious ministers and leaders, who the ANC regarded as powerful allies because of the amount of influence they exercised over their communities. During an address at a meeting of the Ministers' Interdenominational Society of the Western Cape, Mandela cited the example of Afrikaners using the church to promulgate their views, and emphasized that those fighting in the struggle should also take advantage of the churches that were on their side to strengthen their ranks. Mandela would also find inspiration in a prayer by Reverend Japhta, who called on God to assist those in the struggle with a powerful appeal that greatly moved Mandela: "God, we have been praying to you, pleading with you, asking you to liberate us. *Now* we are instructing you to liberate us."[10]

The apartheid government under Hendrik Verwoerd rejected the All-in African Conference's demand for the formulation of a new constitution by a national convention, and on May 31 South Africa became a republic based on the outcome of a whites-only referendum. The NAC was forced to go ahead with the strike, which lasted from May 29 to 31. The stay-away did not draw a large amount of people, and Mandela called it off on the second day, although he would describe the response as a massive success in public.[11] In June, Mandela announced that the ANC would begin a full-scale campaign of non-cooperation with the government of the Republic of South Africa in response to the government's continued refusal to listen to the party's demands.

By now it had become increasingly evident to the ANC that it needed to implement military tactics in its resistance campaign in order for it to be effective. For certain members of the party, however, promoting freedom from oppression through the use of violence was an unappetizing notion. Albert Luthuli, in particular, who was a devout Christian and a believer in Mahatma Gandhi's philosophy of non-violence, voiced his concerns about the party adopting force to advance its aims. While Mandela viewed the use of force as a tactic that would help the ANC to get its point across, and that could be abandoned if conditions called for it, Luthuli, according to Mandela, perceived the ANC's non-violent position as a matter of principle.[12]

Mandela, like Luthuli, was a product of a Christian upbringing and education, but he kept his religious beliefs separate from what he viewed as a political struggle for freedom from apartheid. In his opinion, ideology was something that needed to be combined with practicality and considered in context. "If the adoption of non-violence gave it that effectiveness, that efficiency, we would pursue non-violence. But if the condition shows that non-violence was not effective, we would use other means," he said of the motivations behind endorsing the armed struggle.[13] Mandela viewed Jesus Christ as someone else who had employed force to drive a point forward, as he had done when he confronted money-changers in a synagogue. For Mandela, peaceful methods were inadequate in the struggle when violence was the only means of getting one's message across.[14]

Luthuli, in contrast, ascribed precedence to his faith before his belief in any other ideal or philosophy, and this was what informed every political decision he made. Speaking of his approach to the way he integrated politics into his religious life, Luthuli had said, "I am in Congress precisely because I am a Christian. My Christian belief about society must find expression here and now, and

Congress is the spearhead of the real struggle.... My own urge, because I am a Christian, is to get into the thick of the struggle with
other Christians, taking my Christianity with me and praying that it
may be used to influence for good the character of the resistance."[15]

In the fight for freedom, it was inevitable, in Luthuli's view, that
there would be individuals and groups who had to take the lead
and suffer as a result. "The Road to Freedom is via the Cross," he
had once declared.[16] Another reference to Luthuli's conviction that
his faith drove his participation in the struggle is in the title of his
biography, *Let My People Go*. This, his biographer Scott Couper
argues, is a fundamentally biblical rather than political title; one
that draws comparisons between Luthuli and the biblical hero
Moses, who led the Jews out of Egypt. Luthuli, Couper says, saw
himself as the kind of ethical political leader that Moses was – a
non-violent and non-militaristic activist who would lead his people
away from tyranny without becoming a tyrant himself. Luthuli,
Couper indicates, was of the opinion that he was a spiritual leader
far more than he was a political leader.[17]

But to Mandela, a "consummate politician,"[18] such a principle
held no ground in a matter as sweeping and significant as achieving
freedom for apartheid's subjugated masses. There was no use, he
believed, in chaining oneself to the principle of non-violence when
it would not get one anywhere.[19] Luthuli eventually gave in to this
argument, but he was still adamant that the ANC continue to
pursue non-violent approaches to opposing apartheid, and, for this
reason, suggested that the ANC's military wing be kept separate
and independent from the party's main branch. Mandela recalled
how Luthuli framed this proposal to him: "Very well, you have
made a case. We give you permission. You can go and start this

organization. That is you, Mandela, you can go and start this organization ... and you can join with others and so on: collaborate with others, cooperate with others." Luthuli had given the go-ahead for the formation of *Umkhonto we Sizwe* (MK), but in singling out Mandela and the "others" who would join him in the initiative, his consent sounded more like an admonishment than a declaration of support. He also made a point of elucidating what area of ANC politics he supported: "We as the ANC, we are formed to prosecute a non-violent policy; this decision can only be changed by a national conference. We are going to stick to the old policy of the ANC."[20] With this pronouncement, the president of the ANC handed over all responsibility for the armed struggle to Mandela.

In later years, Luthuli apparently stated that Mandela had not consulted him about the formation of MK, but Mandela disputed this allegation. He recalled both Luthuli's opposition to the armed struggle, and his subsequent approval of the scheme at a meeting in June 1961, during which he had said, "Well my comrades, we have taken this decision. We have taken this decision that we must start violence and establish an army, but I would like to appeal to you: let's take our original positions." Following that statement, discussions about the matter continued throughout the night. Mandela concluded, "So for him to say that we didn't consult him was just the fact that he was ill and he forgot very easily.... But the matter was thoroughly debated."[21]

Thereafter, a policy of armed struggle by the ANC was formalized and Mandela was named the commander-in-chief of *Umkhonto we Sizwe* (Spear of the Nation), the wing of the party which would carry out the struggle's militant activities. The ANC would, at the same time, and through Luthuli's insistence, continue to pursue a policy of non-violence in its endeavor to achieve a democratic South Africa.

On Saturday, December 16, 1961, the ANC's armed struggle against the apartheid government commenced with the detonation of home-made bombs in Johannesburg, Durban and Port Elizabeth, at locations that included an electrical substation and the offices of the Bantu Administration Board.[22] The date held a special place in Afrikaner history as the "Day of the Covenant," marking the anniversary of the Voortrekkers' victory over the Zulu army led by Dingaan in 1838 in the Battle of Blood River. Before the battle, the Voortrekkers had made a covenant with God that a church would be built in his honor if they were victorious.[23] By launching its military campaign on this day, the ANC was therefore making a powerful statement about the God who the Afrikaners had summoned on their side in their war against the Zulu army. Following the attacks, Mandela released a statement that summed up the changed situation of resistance politics in the country: "The time comes in the time of any nation when there remains only two choices – submit or fight. That time has now come to South Africa. We shall not submit and we have no choice but to hit back by all means within our power in defense of our people, our future and our freedom."[24] The strength and conviction in this statement, with its declaration of war against a seemingly unbeatable enemy, seemed to mark Mandela as a prophet who had come forward to make his own covenant – one that called for a change in the system of racial inequality undermining the biblical principle that all people were made in God's image. This same God, Mandela seemed to be saying, would now be exacting his justice on behalf of the oppressed peoples of apartheid South Africa.

6

An Imprisonment of the Spirit

I N JANUARY 1962, the ANC illegally sent Mandela to Addis Ababa, Ethiopia, to attend the Pan-African Freedom Movement of East and Central Africa. This movement mobilized the struggle for independence in that part of the continent. In the same year, Mandela received some military training in Morocco with Algerian freedom fighters and then visited Oliver Tambo in London, where the secretary general of the ANC was living in exile and leading the international chapter of the party. Mandela quietly returned to South Africa in July 1962, during which time he visited Winnie, before setting out for Natal in the same month. It was on this journey, following sixteen months of underground activities, that he was arrested at a police roadblock on the afternoon of August 5, 1962, and taken to Johannesburg to appear in court on charges of inciting black workers and leaving South Africa unlawfully. A despondent Winnie met him in the public gallery during his court appearance and visited him again days later at the Old Fort prison, where a compassionate guard averted his eyes as they held onto each other. "We embraced and clung to each other with all the strength and pent-up emotion inside each of us, as if this was to be the final parting. In a way, it was for we were to be separated for much longer than either of us could then have imagined," Mandela later said of this encounter.[1]

The trial was moved to Pretoria, where Mandela mounted his own defense and chose not to contest the charges against him or to call any witnesses. He was less concerned with arguing for his individual freedom than with using the trial as a space to promote the political agenda of the ANC.[2] On November 7, 1962, the day after the United Nations voted for the first time to impose sanctions on South Africa, Mandela was sentenced to five years' hard labor without any possibility of parole in a move that demonstrated the state's determination to suppress all would-be insurrectionists.

But the government was not finished with the Mandelas. Following his conviction, Mandela was held in virtual isolation for the first few months of his imprisonment and was not allowed any visitors or letters. Three days after Christmas 1962, Winnie was banned and restricted to the Johannesburg magisterial district, and banned from being quoted by the media and attending meetings. In a brutal display of power, the apartheid government had found ways of preventing both husband and wife from participating in any revolutionary activities. When Mandela was suddenly moved, without warning, to Robben Island in May 1963, his engagement with political matters became virtually impossible. The way the transfer was carried out was a telling indication of the treatment the Mandelas would receive for the rest of his imprisonment. Winnie was given no notice of her husband's transfer, and arriving as usual to visit him at Pretoria Central Prison, she was told that he was no longer being held there, but was given no information as to where he had been moved. Forced to discover this information for herself, she would only end up seeing him a month later.[3]

Mandela's initial stay on Robben Island was a short one. On June 12 he was returned to prison in Pretoria. On July 11, 1963, the police raided the ANC's headquarters at Liliesleaf Farm in Rivonia, Johannesburg, and found a number of documents implicating him in MK activities. Many other notable ANC members were arrested too, including Walter Sisulu, Govan Mbeki, Ahmed Kathrada, Arthur Goldreich, Elias Motsoaledi, Andrew Mlangeni, Raymond Mhlaba, Rusty Bernstein and Denis Goldberg. Mandela joined his fellow accused on charges of conspiracy and sabotage in what became known as the Rivonia Trial. There were fears that they would all be executed, but their lives were spared and they were given life sentences.

Mandela's return to Robben Island to serve his life sentence marked a new period in his life and redefined his role in the struggle against apartheid. He could no longer be an active participant in ANC politics, but had to endure this time in prison as a sacrifice for the struggle that had possessed him so entirely for nearly two decades. Mandela was forty-five years old when Robben Island was decreed his new home, and while the first half of his life had seen him fight back against the wrongs perpetrated by the apartheid government, the second half of his existence – all of which he expected to spend in prison – would have him endure these injustices with fortitude and acceptance. The isolation and emptiness that defined Mandela's imprisonment on the island represented a new test of the spirit.

Robben Island was indeed an ideal place to banish political activists who had caused enough trouble on the mainland to warrant their removal from South African society. Separated from the African continent by seven kilometers of Atlantic Ocean, the island is usually the first bit of land to face the biting winds and ferocious

storms that batter Cape Town. For those political prisoners condemned to serve their sentences there, Robben Island provided
ample opportunity to come to terms with the toll that their imprisonment would wreak on them, body and spirit. Catching a glimpse
of ships passing by or of the occasional visitor to the island was
usually the only contact the prisoners had with the world from
which they had been banished.

During Mandela's time on Robben Island, the prison staff and
their families used a magnificent Anglican church, the Church
of the Good Shepherd – built in 1895 by lepers who lived on
the island – as a Dutch Reformed church. The prisoners could see
the church from the prison, but were never allowed to use it. For
inmates such as Winston Njongonkulu Ndungane, this was just
one of the many ways in which Robben Island's prison deprived its
inmates of any meaningful social interaction with one another and
the rest of the world. In democratic South Africa, Ndungane would
succeed Archbishop Desmond Tutu as leader of Southern Africa's
Anglican community, his time in office coinciding with Mandela's
term as president. During his imprisonment on Robben Island,
however, he was forced to watch every Sunday as white residents on
the island, mostly South African Prison Services employees, attended
the same church in which he had been raised, and from which he
was now barred.

Born in Kokstad in 1941, Ndungane's family had served in the
Anglican Church for two generations; both his father and his grandfather had been ministers. Ndungane, though, initially chose not to
seek a career in religion, distinguishing himself instead in liberation
politics as a young recruit in Robert Sobukwe's breakaway party,
the PAC. Sobukwe's militant and visionary approach to the freedom

struggle, along with his natural charisma, eloquence and directness, resonated with Ndungane, who as a young boy growing up in the township of Langa in Cape Town had been more interested in playing football than inciting revolution in South Africa. Sobukwe made a faithful follower out of Ndungane, winning him over by educating him and his friends in the ways apartheid infiltrated every aspect of black society, even to the point of controlling how black people could move about in the country of their birth. Sobukwe's eloquent depiction of the pass laws as being at the center of the apartheid government's oppression of black people in South Africa inspired Ndungane in 1960 to advance the PAC's radical message and to help raise awareness among Langa residents about the atrocities of apartheid. His political activities soon got him arrested and convicted on charges of being a member of a banned party, and he was sentenced to three years' hard labor on Robben Island with no chance of remission.

Ndungane's experiences on the island provide a good comparison for the kind of anguish and spiritual torment Mandela endured during his own time there. For many of the prisoners, the trials during their detention were distressing enough to make them question or even disown their long-held beliefs in a political cause or religion. The prison authorities used degradation and abuse to crush the spirit and character of their prisoners. Ndungane recalls the boat ride transporting him to the island, during which he and the seven other PAC supporters who were sentenced with him were handcuffed in pairs and placed in leg irons before being kicked in the back by the warder into the boat's hold, where they had to synchronize their actions in order to avoid falling.[4]

When prisoners landed on Robben Island, they were usually

preyed upon by warders who took pleasure in telling them that they would never be released from their prison. The warders also encouraged ordinary inmates to intimidate and terrorize the new arrivals, especially those sentenced to Robben Island for political reasons. Prisoners who were members of the radical PAC elicited the particular contempt of the prison guards and were treated more cruelly than the other political prisoners. Educated inmates were also targets, and were frequently humiliated and beaten by men envious of their schooling. Many of the prison guards felt that the isolation on the island, as well as the nature of many of the prisoners' so-called crimes, gave them license to be cruel. In their view, they were helping to punish the terrorists who had tried to break the system that upheld white privilege and power, believing that they were ultimately participating in the same fight as their government. It was a situation that provided enough anguish to break even the strongest of wills.

Ndungane arrived on Robben Island in 1963, the same year as his mentor Sobukwe and a year before Mandela was given his life sentence. Ndungane was immediately put to work in the building crew that had to quarry the stone for one of the island's jails. "I always say my claim to fame is that I built Mandela's jail," Ndungane remarks of his work on the island, "because Mandela came afterwards. We were involved in the building operation of Mandela's prison. He came in 1964. We were there in 1963."[5]

Ndungane notes the subtle form of "torture" enacted on the prisoners by having them build the same walls that would imprison them. It was daily abuses of this kind, and the evident disregard shown towards the humanity of the island's prisoners, that forced a man with such strong links to the Anglican Church to question his own beliefs. "I think I wrestled with God ... how can a good God have about 1,500 of us [imprisoned on Robben Island] when actually we are fighting a just cause.... Why does a good God allow all of this to happen to us?"[6]

These were no doubt questions that many political prisoners with religious beliefs asked themselves on Robben Island, including Mandela.

The constant pressures that were placed on the morale of the prisoners were no doubt exacerbated by the lack of spiritual sustenance on the island. In the twenty months that Ndungane served at the prison, he witnessed neither a religious service nor a visit from a priest or any other kind of spiritual leader. The isolation on the island – from other people and from the religious services and sacraments that helped to affirm and uphold their beliefs – eventually began to change each prisoner's individual relationship with God. Whether the result of this changed relationship was a loss of faith and subsequent despair, or a strengthening in beliefs and an accompanying sense of hope, depended on how they eventually coped with their spiritual isolation. Ndungane chose to seek solace and friendship in his fellow political prisoners, who, like him, ultimately understood that their incarceration was serving a greater purpose than one that could be achieved on an individual level.

Through this solidarity and the "knowledge that our cause was just," Ndungane and his friends eventually realized that they had reached a defining moment in their struggle for liberation. The prayers they said together every evening, and their recital of "Nkosi Sikelel' iAfrika", helped them feel as if their own moment of liberation was soon approaching.[7]

* * *

Now excluded from political activism and far away from Winnie and his children, Mandela, like Ndungane, was acutely aware of the fact that he was fighting a new battle – one that sought to take as its prize the soul of every political activist imprisoned on Robben Island. By keeping the likes of Mandela and Sobukwe alienated from the rest of their political allies in South Africa, and ensuring that they had no means whatsoever of participating in the struggle, the apartheid government had found a way not only to prevent these activists from causing any more trouble, but to remove them completely from the struggle narrative. By limiting family visits to a mere half hour once a year and prohibiting the media from publishing anything about the prisoners, the authorities further alienated them from society.

As a boy, Mandela had heard stories about the Xhosa chief Makana's imprisonment on the island, and how he had drowned as he attempted to escape.[8] Now Mandela was in the same situation as his rebellious tribesman and would have to learn to cope with the pain of his own incarceration without succumbing to Makana's fate. One way he did this was through work on the island, which to him, though challenging, "had its own sense of joy." While he worked, Mandela enjoyed looking out at the sea and at all the other natural features that animated the island, such as the rock formations and the birds that lived there. "Nature came to be very important for me," he later recalled. "It sustained, invigorated and inspired me." The companionship of the other prisoners, especially of his fellow Rivonia trialists, provided another kind of joy and hope. With the knowledge that they would probably all be sharing the same tiny living space for the rest of their lives, they found themselves growing together as men as the years went by, and the harsh reality of their imprisonment became easier to accept: "those were tough but formative years which we spent together," Mandela said of the time he spent in prison with his comrades.[9]

The rest of the Rivonia black collective, who were in a sense exiled to Robben Island (unlike Goldberg, who was jailed in Pretoria), were also wise to the government's campaign to silence them and to discredit any influence they might have exercised outside of prison. Ahmed Kathrada, who was sentenced to life in prison along with Mandela, maintains that it was for this reason that Mandela encouraged inmates to attend the services of religious representatives whenever they were allowed to visit the island. While some political prisoners with shorter prison sentences – like Ndungane – never received such visits, they could at least attend church services and obtain religious guidance once they were released from prison. But for the Rivonia trialists, condemned to spend the rest of their lives on the island, any occasion to converse with a religious leader was a privilege, and Mandela understood this. Like his father and his great-grandfather before him, Mandela used religion as a means of resisting the exclusionary tactics of the system that kept the prisoners separated from the rest of the world. Listening to the sermons of religious leaders and participating in the rituals of a religion, the tenets of which transcend the boundaries of race and class, helped to remind the prisoners that they still had a place in a civilized world – where ideas such as love and freedom were venerated – even while they were excluded. This might have been why Mandela's religious beliefs seemed to strengthen in prison, as he had previously dedicated most of his time to politics. Religion could help to soothe the conflicts that raged among members of a group or unsettled the mind of the individual. Mandela later admitted that he turned constantly to religion on Robben Island: "I never missed a service and often read the scripture lessons.... Come to think of it, I was quite religious."[10]

Kathrada points out that for many of Robben Island's inmates who never received visitors and only ever encountered non-convicts in the form of prison guards, a visit from a religious leader was an opportunity to see a new face and to learn about what was going on in the outside world. Sometimes a free-thinking or more courageous priest would even agree to convey information about an inmate to his family or friends. Mandela singled out Father Alan Hughes of the Anglican Church as a religious visitor to the island who helped the prisoners remember that the world continued to spin outside the walls that separated them from it. "He was always willing to share pieces of information denied to us on the island," Mandela said of Father Hughes. "He helped us keep in touch with the wider community, locating his religious message within the broader context of life. His religion was an impressive spiritual understanding of life – never something separate from it."[11]

Kathrada remembers Father Hughes as a "lovely old man" who was the favorite priest of the Robben Island prisoners. His services at the prison attracted inmates from all religions, even atheists, Hindus and Muslims, and Mandela shared their affection for the minister – although Father Hughes would frequently confuse him with fellow political prisoner Fikile Bam because the two men were the same height. In his interactions with the prisoners, Father Hughes generally knew what they needed to hear and was able to develop a rapport with them. This characteristic could be credited to the fact that he had experience ministering to prisoners in prisoner-of-war camps during the Second World War.[12] For

Mandela, Father Hughes's sermons were so important because "[w]hat he said not only enriched the spirit, but more, it left me full of hope."[13]

At times, ministers provided prisoners with information about the world they had left behind entirely by accident. Kathrada remembers an incident in which two prisoners, Eddie Daniels and Hennie Ferrus, relieved a Brother September of his newspaper during one of his services by tricking him into closing his eyes for a prayer, which Ferrus was leading. With Brother September's eyes closed in concentration, Daniels was able to steal his paper. It was one of the rare occasions when the prisoners could discover what was going on in the rest of South Africa. To them, procuring a newspaper was comparable to a free man discovering a huge pile of gold. Nevertheless, with limited family visits, censored mail – both incoming and outgoing – and only one another for company, the prisoners had to be careful in their dealings with religious leaders, as the slightest offense on the part of either could end all further visits. Brother September therefore made sure never to bring a newspaper with him again – a fact which Kathrada found amusing all the same.

As the youngest and most impressionable of the Rivonia accused on the island, Kathrada, like Mandela and Sisulu, attended as many religious services held in Robben Island's prison as he could. For Mandela, doing this was also a way of showing "respect to the individual and the religion itself: to the individual because even when the seas were rough they [religious leaders] used to come. They were our window to the world, really," says Kathrada.[14]

In the beginning, prisoners remained in their cells, each of which housed only one inmate, during church services. The prison guards would unlock the wooden door of each cell while keeping its metal gate secured, and the priest would stand at the entrance of the passage leading to the cells. Warders would attend the services as well, and sermons had to stick to subjects of a strictly religious nature. If their sermons took a political detour, ministers would be banned from preaching to the prisoners.

Peter Storey was one such minister who Kathrada realized must have been "too political for the authorities" at the prison. A priest in the Methodist Church, Storey seemed to possess the same vigor and desire to spread the message of his religion to those he believed were in desperate need of spiritual enlightenment as his nineteenth-century predecessor, William Shaw.

Storey had a tendency to express his opinions rather candidly. While many people could be taken aback by his openness, it marked him as a person of integrity, and a good candidate for ministering to people who were considered outcasts by the rest of South African society. The prisoners could depend on him to be upfront about what was really going on in the outside world, unlike a minister who was too afraid of angering the prison authorities.

In 1963, Peter Storey was still a young, inexperienced priest at the Camps Bay Methodist church when he volunteered to minister to prisoners on Robben Island. His superior, Bishop Derrick Timm, had asked if anyone among his staff was willing to be a chaplain there. Storey's reasons for wanting to go to the island were initially neither straightforward nor magnanimous. "The reason ... was really because I had been in the navy and had very unwillingly obeyed a call to the ministry," says Storey. "But I was missing being on the water. And so I thought, here is a chance to get on the boats again."[15]

While being back on the sea was exhilarating for Storey, he

could not relate to the rest of the passengers on the boat taking him to the island. Most were prison staff, while the rest were visitors. A sense of camaraderie seemed to unite them all, but it was an atmosphere from which Storey felt excluded because he held a very different view about the people he was to minister to. "You felt alienated, you were not part of them," he remembers. "You were not part of the culture of the prison warders. And you did not want to be. And you had in your mind the fact that this is the boat that carried prisoners in shackles … that it was really the boat that delivered people to their doom if you like. So it was a horrible thing.... I loved being at sea. I still do. But you realized you were part of something very ugly. And it left its mark on you."[16]

Storey did not know that political prisoners were being held on Robben Island. It was only in 1964, after he had presided over services for regular prisoners for about a year, that the warders informed him that he would have to minister to the "other prisoners" too. The Rivonia trialists had just arrived and Nelson Mandela was one of the inmates Storey would have under his care. He was, however, unaware of Mandela's presence throughout the time he ministered on the island.

During the services he presided over for the Rivonia prisoners, Storey walked up and down the passageway, peering into the cells while he spoke – an experience he describes as both terrible and surreal. Not allowed to communicate one-on-one with any of the prisoners, Storey preached his sermon as he moved through the passageway, and tried to connect with the men despite the impersonal and unconventional nature of the church service. "It was very difficult to conduct a service and worship that way," he says. "I developed a way of trying to engage each person's eyes as I passed."[17]

The prisoners sometimes sang hymns, and Storey recalls how pleasing it was to hear the passion and joy in their voices as they remembered their favorites. Only Kathrada, as a Muslim, was unfamiliar with the songs, while Govan Mbeki, an atheist, showed the least interest in Storey's sermons.

In his interactions with the warders, Storey found that being white often led them to assume that he shared their views of the prisoners as the rightful captives of the apartheid government. Storey initially ate lunch in the canteen with the warders, but after some time he started bringing his own lunch with him, which he ate alone, as he found their opinions distasteful and unacceptable.

Nevertheless, Storey – who would go on to head the Methodist Church as well as the South African Council of Churches (SACC) in the early 1980s – is deeply grateful that he was given the opportunity to minister to Mandela and the other brave men who gave up their freedom in the fight against apartheid: "Even if there had been no political prisoners, even if these were common-law prisoners, the fact that you were given entrance in these people's lives and you were permitted to bring a word of humanity in a very inhuman situation … did place an important responsibility on your shoulders … it was a great privilege, and when I began to understand who these people were that I was asked to minister to, I did have a sense of the significance of those moments."[18]

Of his own church, Storey feels that the Wesleyans' time-honored practice of spreading their message even to those condemned to live on the margins of society was the reason why so many of apartheid's political prisoners could receive spiritual nourishment while behind bars. Storey explains why the church places this emphasis on catering to the spiritual needs of the world's outcasts:

"One of the things that John Wesley said was that you must go not only to those who need you, but [to] those who need you most ... unless you are visiting the prisoner and the naked and ... the insignificant and the poor, you are going to miss out on Jesus himself." Storey considers tending to the Methodists' most needy flock in prison to be the inescapable and preordained duty of any person who chooses to be a servant of the church. He acknowledges that the state recognized this aspect of the church's doctrine to some degree and was at least willing to appoint chaplains nominated by the church to serve prisons, even if the government did reserve the right to remove anyone from their post if they were viewed as insubordinate or non-conformist.[19]

For Storey, this punishment came six months into his tenure as minister to the Rivonia trialists, soon after he had preached a sermon to the inmates that the prison authorities considered objectionable. Having managed to persuade the guards to allow the inmates to hear his sermon in the courtyard outside their cells, where the sun was shining brightly on all their faces, Storey overstepped a line when he said that one day the real son, the son of God, would set them free. Soon afterwards, his security clearance was withdrawn and he received a letter in the post from the Department of Prisons telling him that he could no longer minister to prisoners on Robben Island.[20] The prison authorities probably viewed Storey's words as being too subversive. They could not risk anyone conditioning their prisoners to believe that they were free from prison rule, even in a spiritual sense.

After Storey's visits ended, the prisoners continued to attend religious services in the courtyard on Sundays. For those in solitary confinement, these services were a welcome relief from the loneliness and seclusion of their punishment.

Kathrada remembers a time when he and Govan Mbeki were both in solitary confinement – Kathrada for six months and Mbeki for three. Although Mbeki was an atheist, he would often beg Kathrada to request that a priest be sent to them, as they would then be allowed to go outside. "He'd say, 'Please ask for the priest,'" Kathrada remembers. "I used to say, 'No, I'm not a Christian, I'm not an Anglican, I'm not a Methodist, how can I ask?' But I was teasing him. I used to ask. That was the only time he came [to services] because he was in solitary confinement. You want to be out in the sun to warm yourselves."[21]

Kathrada provides other humorous anecdotes of inmates swarming to listen to the sermons of religious leaders in order to break the monotony of being in prison and, at times, of even pretending to be part of a religion so that they could get certain privileges. One prisoner who tried his luck was M.D. Naidoo, a member of the SACP and the husband of Phyllis Naidoo, who had declared himself an atheist when he was imprisoned on the island. When a Hindu priest bearing delicious food for Diwali came to visit the inmates, Naidoo, along with a few other prisoners, pretended to be Hindu. When the warders asked Naidoo, who demanded to visit the courtyard to see his priest, what church he was a part of, Naidoo responded that he was not part of a church but of a temple. He was therefore allowed to visit with the Hindu priest and ended up enjoying himself immensely. Many of the prisoners also looked forward to the visits of one member of the clergy who was somehow allowed to serve wine during Holy Communion. When he was eventually forced to use orange juice, "the congregation [size] went down," Kathrada chuckles.[22]

Even though religious leaders from a variety of religions visited the island, Christian ministers formed the majority, as most of the inmates were Christian. It was only in 1978 that Kathrada and the rest of the island's Muslim inmates received a visit from an imam. Imam Abdurahman Bassier was one of the most respected religious leaders in his community, and had ministered to Muslim patients in hospitals for thirteen years before he applied to serve Muslim prisoners on Robben Island. Bassier was given an hour on the island and told that he could only minister to people of his own faith. But after meeting two common-law Muslim prisoners (one of whom was so happy to see a different face on the island that he embraced the imam until it hurt), Bassier was given the opportunity to visit the maximum-security block and meet Kathrada and two of his fellow Rivonia trialists – Walter Sisulu and Nelson Mandela.

The prison had mandated that Bassier speak only to Kathrada, but he could not bear to do so when other members of the Rivonia group were eager to meet him and talk to him about the world outside the prison. The meeting took up so much of his time that he was unable to complete his ministration to Kathrada.

Later, on the deck of the *Dias*, the ferry returning him to Cape Town, Bassier reflected on his visit with the men on Robben Island, marvelling at how fit and healthy they looked, and how undefeated they seemed, despite being aware that they would most likely die there.

For the next three years the imam regularly visited this group of religiously diverse men, and Mandela had fond memories of their exchanges: "I particularly enjoyed the visits of Imam Abdurahman Bassier with whom I had long conversations," Mandela said. "It was an enriching experience for me to gain a deeper knowledge of a religion other than my own."[23] Bassier's visits to the island eventually ended when he, like Storey, seemed to forget for a moment where he was and told the prisoners that "it seemed such a pity that so much knowledge was stored in so small an area, while the rest of the country was in such need of it." Even though he was referring to a topic unrelated to that of the political situation, the warders wrote Bassier up, and on his next visit he was escorted to a room where he was allowed to meet only Muslim inmates. In 1982, when some of the Rivonia prisoners were transferred to Pollsmoor, Bassier was told a rather dubious story that prison policy prevented a religious leader who had already ministered to inmates in one prison from doing so once they had been moved to another.[24]

Kathrada remembers Bassier fondly, recalling that the prisoners once asked him to "convey our situation to the outside world" when they were on one of their hunger strikes. The prisoners knew that the rest of South Africa was not aware of the conditions under which they were living on Robben Island, and so the imam became an important ally in informing the world about their plight. He and Mandela would share an admiration for each other that lasted throughout their lifetimes, and Bassier was one of the many religious leaders who was sure, after meeting Mandela in prison, that he was destined to lead South Africa out of apartheid. When Mandela was eventually released, he visited the imam's mosque in the Bo-Kaap in March 1992, both in an attempt to garner votes from the Muslim community in the area, and to show his appreciation to them for their participation in the struggle. When Bassier died in 2004, Mandela sent his family a letter of condolence.[25]

Mandela's encounters with religious representatives on Robben Island clearly had a lasting effect on him, even after his release. He would remember the spiritual sermons and counsel of the ministers who visited the prison long after he became president of South Africa, recalling how they had helped him to survive the many stretched-out hours of his incarceration. Having learned as a student the capability of religious leaders to influence the way people thought and behaved, on Robben Island he channelled this same power to hold on to the memory of his other life, the one that still existed far away from the isolation and loneliness he suffered every day.

7

The Sacrament Behind Bars

I N MARCH 1982, after eighteen years on Robben Island, Mandela was transferred to Pollsmoor Prison in Cape Town. He was accompanied by fellow Rivonia prisoners Walter Sisulu, Raymond Mhlaba and Andrew Mlangeni. Kathrada would join the group in October.

Having lived on Robben Island for so long, Mandela found it difficult to leave the prison. He had forged a life for himself there, even if it was devoid of the experiences that people living in regular society take for granted. Prison life had given Mandela a sense of structure and stability, and it was hard for him to let go of that in the face of a new and unknown situation. As he set foot on the ferry that would take him back to Cape Town, he felt overwhelmed by the knowledge that he was leaving the prison that had become his home: "I looked back at the island as the light was fading, not knowing whether I would ever see it again. A man can get used to anything, and I had grown used to Robben Island."[1]

But now Mandela, who was nearly sixty-four years old, would have to acclimatize to the much improved conditions at Pollsmoor Prison. From 1984 onwards, unlike on Robben Island, he was allowed more frequent visits from his family.[2]

On the religious side of things, though, matters actually deteriorated somewhat. On Robben Island, Mandela had been able to meet and converse with a variety of religious leaders from all kinds of faiths. At Pollsmoor, however, prisoners could only have contact with ministers from their own religion or church. Mandela described this as "a source of great disappointment" to him.[3] He was no longer able to witness first-hand the way people of other faiths carried out their worship, which had always been an enriching learning experience for him.

One of the Christian ministers who served Mandela during his time at Pollsmoor was Harry Wiggett, an Anglican priest. Wiggett had first met Mandela in 1968 when he was a young deacon employed to accompany the aging Father Alan Hughes to Robben Island. Wiggett did this job for a few months, and during this time he had the opportunity to observe how skillfully Hughes dealt with the prisoners under his care, and the effort he put into motivating them to continue looking towards the future. When Wiggett found out that a few of those prisoners were now in a prison situated in his parish of Bergvliet, he felt a responsibility to take up Father Hughes's former position as spiritual counselor to these men. His knowledge of who they were and how much they had already contributed to the struggle against apartheid further heightened his sense of duty. So when, in 1982, Wiggett received a phone call from Pollsmoor's commanding officer, Brigadier Fred Munro, asking him to minister to the prison's political inmates, he jumped at the opportunity to serve the men who had given up so much of their lives for the liberation of other people.

On his first morning on the job, Wiggett met with Mandela, Sisulu, Mhlaba, Kathrada and Mlangeni. Mandela, who had not seen Wiggett for almost twenty years, surprised him by asking after his wife, Jean, and their children, Michael and David.

The prisoners attended Wiggett's services, where he administered Holy Communion, as often as they could. A prison warder,
usually Christo Brand – who had worked on Robben Island when
the Rivonia trialists were imprisoned there – sat in on the services
to make sure that Wiggett, considered subversive because he was
part of the *Engelse kerk*, stuck to strictly religious subject matter
during his sermons.[4] Brand also had to ensure that the prisoners
did not misbehave, either by asking ministers to carry messages for
them outside of the prison or by discussing anything besides religion
with the ministers. Brand recalls a few occasions when he caught
Mandela, in particular, trying to break these rules: "Specifically
at Pollsmoor," Brand says, "I had to address him and say, 'Mandela, now you're deviating from the topic. We're here for religious purposes and not for you to send a message through one
pastor to another.'"[5]

Wiggett's instruction book from Pollsmoor stated that he was
not allowed to bring any alcohol into the prison, but his superior
in the Anglican Church, Archbishop Philip Russell, had insisted
that Wiggett take wine with him in order to properly administer the
sacrament of Holy Communion. This caused him some anxiety
during his first service when Brand, at Mandela's insistence, participated. Wiggett remembers the occasion: "[Mandela] said to Brand,
who was sitting right next to me,... 'Are you a Christian?' When
Brand replied that he was, Mandela countered, 'Now look, Brand,
if you're a Christian, you must take off your cap and you must join
us. This is a Christian service.'"[6]

Brand "had no option," in Wiggett's words, but to listen to the
prisoner he had been tasked with watching over. To Wiggett, this
occasion was proof of Mandela's profound spirituality – of his

capacity to see beyond the surface appearance or behavior of any person and to recognize within them an individual who possessed beliefs and ideas just as he did. Wiggett states that even though he was a religious servant, he had not taken this into consideration when he had met the warder: "I had branded Brand. He was NGK, he was Dutch Reformed, he was a nationalist, he was right-wing, he was irrelevant. But not to Nelson. [To Mandela], he was a person as much in need of the grace and love of God as anyone else, and especially when we were celebrating Jesus and the death of Jesus.... I think it was one of the most important life-changing spiritual experiences that I've undergone. Here the priest had already judged the other man, excluded him, which our churches do. We are very exclusive, and the prisoner, who is a danger to everyone, is a liberator, and this is in 1982."[7]

But now Wiggett had to worry about what would happen when Brand discovered that real wine was being served during the sacrament. However, when Brand's turn came to drink from the chalice holding the wine, nothing happened; the service continued as usual. Mandela had pointed out to Brand that he was just like the other prisoners attending the service – a Christian – and so he behaved as such, showing the necessary respect for the sacraments in which he was participating.

Wiggett and Mandela became good friends at Pollsmoor, and Wiggett was able to learn about and contribute to the other man's spiritual growth. The strength of Mandela's spiritual beliefs made such an impression on Wiggett that, in 1985, when this aspect of the future president's character was put under fire in the media, Wiggett rose to Mandela's defense.[8]

The year 1985 was a turbulent one for South Africa. The country was shaken by numerous anti-government demonstrations, loud calls to free Nelson Mandela and pressures from outside the country for the apartheid government to effect political change. In January, the government had offered to release Mandela from prison on the condition that he publicly denounce the use of violence in the struggle. But Mandela naturally rejected what was clearly an attempt by the state to make him its puppet.[9] In July, President P.W. Botha declared a state of emergency that allowed for the arbitrary detention without trial of thousands of people and increased police brutality. And yet, even in the face of all of this opposition, the apartheid government continued to claim that Mandela was a man of violence, a communist and a non-believer.

Although determined to stay true to the ANC and his own principles, it was difficult for Mandela to express to the public what he truly believed while he was locked up in Pollsmoor. As he was restricted from giving interviews to the media, he had become easy prey for people seeking to promote their own political agendas, and who were happy to take advantage of the fact that he could not defend himself in public. This was nowhere better illustrated than in August 1985, when President Botha gave special permission to two American journalists from the *Washington Times*, John Lofton and Cal Thomas, to interview Mandela.

Fred Munro, who was present at the interview, recalls Mandela telling the Americans that there was "no alternative to taking up arms" in the struggle against apartheid. He remembers that they also interrogated Mandela about his religious beliefs, and accused him of being a communist. Eventually, Munro says, Mandela announced to the journalists, "I am a Methodist. I've always been a Methodist."[10]

The statement came as a surprise to his prison warders, who had not known what Mandela's religious beliefs were before that moment. While on Robben Island, Christo Brand had been aware of Mandela's insistence that other inmates interact with ministers as much as possible, but he had not realized that this was because of any spiritual belief on Mandela's part.[11] Nevertheless, when Mandela's interview was published overseas in the *Washington Times*, it was riddled with distortions about his religious and political beliefs, and he had no recourse to set the record straight as there were very few people in South Africa who could publicly speak up for him. Although Fred Munro was present during the interview, prison regulations forbade him from speaking to the media about his charges while they were behind bars.[12]

Mandela later claimed that the journalists seemed committed to promulgating certain ideas about him that would add support to the view that he was a man of violence. Consequently, any attempts by him to explain his motivations for the armed struggle were repeatedly challenged by them, as he later explained:

> They seemed less intent on finding out my views than on proving that I was a Communist and a terrorist. All of their questions were slanted in that direction, and when I reiterated that I was neither a Communist nor a terrorist, they attempted to show that I was not a Christian either by asserting that the Reverend Martin Luther King never resorted to violence. I told them that the conditions in which Martin Luther King struggled were totally different from my own: the United States was a democracy with constitutional guarantees of equal rights that protected nonviolent protest (though there was still

prejudice against blacks); South Africa was a police state with a constitution that enshrined inequality and an army that responded to nonviolence with force.[13]

The *Washington Times* journalists, however, were not convinced, and Mandela later recalled the moment that Fred Munro had witnessed, when he revealed that he "was a Christian and had always been a Christian" – a part of his life that he generally kept private. Mandela used the example of Jesus Christ to clarify his outlook on the armed struggle to the Americans. "He was not a man of violence," Mandela rationalized, "but had no choice but to use force against evil." Eventually, however, Mandela realized that he was fighting a losing battle. "I do not think I persuaded them," he later concluded.[14]

Wiggett was first alerted to the accusations that were being thrown at Mandela by the *Washington Times* when Archbishop Russell told him to read the article after it appeared in the local *Sunday Times* on August 25, 1985.

As Wiggett read the article, he found himself becoming more and more outraged at the claims that were being made about the man he had been ministering to for three years. He questioned the integrity of the journalists who had interviewed Mandela, especially after he recognized one of them, Cal Thomas, as a member of Reverend Jerry Falwell's Moral Majority organization.

Falwell was an American Southern Baptist minister who held very conservative views on a number of subjects, including homosexuality, and who had also opposed sanctions against apartheid South Africa. The Moral Majority was a conservative political party that advocated the philosophy of the American Christian Right.[15] "I read this," Wiggett says of the article, "and I think: 'Good Lord, this is first of all peculiar that one of Jerry Falwell's men should get in and interview Nelson Mandela.' I thought that sounds phony to start with."[16]

Wiggett called Archbishop Russell, who ordered him to immediately report to his official residence in Bishopscourt. When the archbishop asked Wiggett for his impressions of the article, Wiggett responded, "It's not right. This is not the Nelson I'm meeting with. It might have been [him] before he went to prison. But we all grow, we all develop. We all change our viewpoints." For three years, Wiggett had studied scripture with Mandela and ministered to him, and he had come to know Mandela as a gentle and contemplative man – an aspect of the politician's character that many people, even some who had known him for most of his life, did not know existed.

Archbishop Russell asked Wiggett if he would write a response to the article for the *Sunday Times*, refuting the American journalists' allegations against Mandela. Wiggett was at first hesitant to do so because Pollsmoor expressly forbade priests who ministered at the prison from speaking about their religious charges to the media. He quickly changed his mind, however, when he realized that by keeping quiet about what he knew of Mandela he would be allowing untruths to proliferate. This would have gone against what he believed as a Christian and a minister. His reply to Thomas and Lofton's article appeared a week later, on September 1, in the *Sunday Times*. In his response, Wiggett explained what it was like to minister to the political prisoner: "It has been my privilege to do so, and during that time Mr. Mandela has welcomed me as a Christian priest with obvious joy and sincerity and has received Holy

Communion regularly." Given what he knew of Mandela, he wrote that he found it hard to believe that he was a communist.

It was not too long before Wiggett received a phone call from the prison demanding that he report to Pollsmoor the following day.

The next morning, the priest cheerfully kissed his wife good-bye, half joking with her that she knew where he was if he did not return home.[17] Around this time, the police had arrested a number of religious leaders for taking part in anti-apartheid protests, using the state of emergency as an excuse for detaining them without trial. Among those arrested in the Western Cape in 1985 were Dr. Allan Boesak, who was detained the day before he was to lead a march to Pollsmoor to demand the release of Nelson Mandela; Western Cape Council of Churches chairman Lionel Louw; Professor Charles Villa-Vicencio of the Religious Studies Department at the University of Cape Town; and Reverend Richard J. Stevens of the Dutch Reformed Mission Church.[18] Wiggett's concerns about going to Pollsmoor by himself after his letter about Mandela appeared in the *Sunday Times* were therefore justified.

When Wiggett arrived at Pollsmoor, he was subjected to a verbal attack by the enraged chaplain general of the South African Prison Services, Major General A.C. Sephton, who berated him for disobeying prison regulations before suspending him. Wiggett, however, bore no resentment towards the chaplain general. After witnessing Mandela's dealings with Christo Brand during his first meeting with the activist, the minister had begun to consider people who he would usually have been quick to judge or condemn from a different perspective. With this new point of view, he realized that Sephton, even with all the power he held, was someone who had to be pitied rather than feared. "I felt for him," says Wiggett. "You know, he was doing his job. You believe that the Lord has actually led you [to become a] chaplain general, and [that] you are serving God. And this poor man, he thinks he's right." That people like Sephton continued to help sustain a system that kept so many people subjugated, Wiggett recognized, was something that had to be cured through understanding, not hatred. "I must just try to love him," Wiggett thought during the encounter. If "Nelson could love [a] warder, I could love my brother."[19]

Six weeks later, Wiggett got an unexpected phone call from Fred Munro, who informed him that his suspension had been lifted and that he could resume his duties at Pollsmoor. He advised the minister to behave as if nothing had precipitated the encounter with Sephton.

The next time Wiggett saw Archbishop Russell, he received what his superior described as his "reward" for his efforts: a copy of a handwritten letter that Nelson Mandela had written to Russell on March 4, 1985.[20] In the letter, Mandela recalled attending services at the Anglican Church when he lived in Alexandra, even though he was a Methodist. He also mentioned that he had "been so impressed" by members of the Anglican Church, and revealed how much he had appreciated visits from church ministers during his incarceration on Robben Island:

> Apart from our families, who could only see us once every six months, the only other people we could meet were priests. The interest they took in prisoners, especially during the turbulent days of the '60s, was a source of considerable strength.
>
> And, in such an environment, each sermon made us feel

that we had a million friends, a feeling which made us forget the wretchedness which surrounded us.

Of the priests whose services were very popular in those days was the late Fr. Hughes.... What he said not only enriched the spirit, even more, it left one full of hope.[21]

Archbishop Russell showed Wiggett his reply, in which he assured Mandela that his letters had been arriving at the Anglican Church's headquarters in Bishopscourt, before praising him for "the strength of your Christian faith, showing how the presence of God has been very real and near to you even though in prison. But I suppose that has been the mark of the Christian throughout the ages and I am glad that you are one more of those who has drawn strength and consolation from the power and presence of Jesus Christ." He ended the letter by promising to keep Mandela in his prayers.[22]

Someone else who came to the activist's defense at this time was Dudley Moore, the Methodist priest who had ministered to Mandela since his arrival at Pollsmoor three years earlier.

Moore knew that many people were unsure of what kind of person Mandela was, but he never doubted that Mandela was a good man who harbored no violent feelings towards others, and who continued to show his gratitude to people who supported him or showed him kindness, even if they were the guards appointed to watch over him in prison. During his visits, Moore read to Mandela from scripture and other religious texts, provided him with subjects on which to contemplate his spirituality, and administered Holy Communion. Mandela, Moore and a warder were the only people present during these visits, and the highly personal nature of each of these interactions allowed Moore to discover just how religious Mandela really was. He found a man who understood the importance of meditating on scripture and integrating the values and lessons he learned from it into his own way of thinking. Mandela, likewise, admired Moore and received a great deal of comfort from their meetings.[23] For Mandela, these were "an occasion for me to develop a friendship of great importance with Rev. Dudley Moore, the Methodist chaplain. He visited me on a frequent basis and I received Holy Communion from him regularly. To share the sacrament as part of the tradition of my Church was important for me. It gave me a sense of inner quiet and calm. I used to come away from these services feeling a new man."[24]

Like Wiggett, Moore was upset by Thomas and Lofton's article, particularly the claims that Mandela was a violent man, a communist and scornful of religion. Determined that South Africa learn about the man he had come to know during his ministry at Pollsmoor, Moore wrote a letter to the *Weekly Mail* titled "The Nelson Mandela I Know: By His Minister," which was published on September 27, 1985. In the letter, Moore emphasized the peaceful side of Mandela's nature, and how hard he worked at cultivating his spirituality during the religious services he attended:

I have … been Minister and Pastor to Nelson Mandela ever since his transfer to Pollsmoor Prison from Robben Island. I have got to know the man well, and what I know of the man, as I have ministered to him and been ministered to by him, I must share with the people of South Africa.

I have regularly administered the sacrament of Holy Communion to Nelson Mandela. I did so the day before yesterday.

On that occasion, he spent some time in meditation – meditating on the tension that Jesus must have felt in Gethsemane, knowing that he was to be arrested and killed.

His meditation led him to the thought that in South Africa most of those who are arrested do not have that level of tension. There is a well-known Christian booklet of daily scripture readings and meditation called *Faith for Daily Living*.

Nelson Mandela looks forward to receiving his copy of it. It is an important part of his daily life. I do know that Nelson Mandela appreciates all the good wishes people send to him. He also respects the men who have been appointed to guard him in prison. He gets on well with them.

Is he a communist? He is a nationalist, I know. I do not believe that he is a communist. He would probably admit that he is influenced by some of the teachings of Marx; but then those who would condemn him for that should bear in mind that much of Marx's teachings is [*sic*] not exclusive to communism.

The man Mandela that I know just cannot be a communist. I have written this letter because I believe the people of our country ought to know something about the man. What I have written is not what has been reported to me by others. It is my own personal knowledge of the man, Nelson Mandela.[25]

Moore's letter opposed the apartheid government's persistent claim that Mandela's communist affiliations were evidence of his supposed animosity towards Christianity and democracy. The man Moore defended was not the godless defender of a supposedly evil ideology that strove to undermine Christian principles. Rather, Moore described Mandela as a devoted student of the Methodist faith that he had adopted as a child, and someone who worked hard at assimilating the tenets of this faith, including those of tolerance and forgiveness, which he displayed in his relationships with Pollsmoor's prison warders. Mandela "wholly submitted himself to the sacrament," says Ernest Moore, quoting his father Dudley.[26] While the South African Communist Party would confirm in 2013 that Mandela had indeed been a member of the party for a brief time in 1962, this evidently did nothing to weaken his belief in God or the Christian religion.[27] As far as Moore was concerned, Mandela's faith and deep spirituality proved that he was committed to reconciliation in South Africa, despite the National Party government's attempts to undermine him.

The day after his letter was published, Moore was visited by the security police, who told him that he had contravened his privileges and was no longer allowed to minister to prisoners at Pollsmoor. He was, however, reinstated two weeks later when the Methodist Church intervened with the prison authorities on his behalf. Besides resuming his regular prison duties, Moore was also allowed to continue ministering to Mandela.[28]

It is evident from Mandela's dealings with Christian ministers – many of whom became his friends and spoke out on his behalf when others sought to denigrate him – that the Christian church, when it was willing, could be a powerful participant in the politics of the liberation movement. During apartheid, the responses of different religious institutions to the political system were varied. Some churches, such as the Dutch Reformed Church (DRC), found theological reasons to defend apartheid, while others, such as the Methodist Church, were steadfast in their support for the struggle.

Many, however, did very little or nothing at all to speak out on the system's injustices.[29] According to the Truth and Reconciliation Commission, "Some of the major Christian churches gave their blessing to the system of apartheid. And many of its early proponents prided themselves in being Christians. Indeed, the system of apartheid was regarded as stemming from the mission of the church."[30]

At the same time, a number of representatives of different churches stepped forward to fill the leadership void that had formed in certain areas of the struggle following the imprisonment, banishment and/or death of so many anti-apartheid activists. Many of these individuals contributed a great deal to the struggle, particularly Desmond Tutu of the Anglican Church and Allan Boesak, formerly of the Dutch Reformed Church, both of whom rose to prominence locally and internationally. Because of their standing in the religious community, it was difficult for governments of other countries to dismiss the two church leaders' opposition to apartheid. Boesak was appointed president of the World Alliance of Reformed Churches in 1982, and in the same year, in Ottawa, Canada, the organization declared apartheid a heresy. In 1984, Tutu was awarded the Nobel Peace Prize for his opposition to apartheid, and in 1986 he became the first black Anglican archbishop of Cape Town.

The Methodist Church, meanwhile, continued to express its support for the moral correctness of the struggle and its belief that all people are created equal in the eyes of God. Back in 1963, the church had elected Reverend Seth Mokitimi as its first black president. In 1986, while South Africa was still in a state of emergency, the church held its 150th conference in Pietermaritzburg, at which the incoming president, Reverend John Scholtz, headed a discussion on the Methodist Church's position on the nationalist government.

Scholtz was of the firm opinion that the church could not stand back while the apartheid government continued to pass discriminatory policies that undermined the biblical notion that God "made from one man every nation of mankind to live on all the face of the earth."[31]

At the conference, the church adopted twelve resolutions which would form the basis of a manifesto titled "The Crisis in South Africa." Among other things, these resolutions called for the immediate and complete dismantling of apartheid and its replacement with a system of government that considered all South Africans equal; the lifting of the state of emergency; the release of detainees and political prisoners; the unbanning of political organizations; the recognition of civic and political leaders who had the confidence of the black community; and the unequivocal commitment of government to negotiating with these leaders for a new constitution.[32]

The adoption of these resolutions was a significant event in the history of the Methodist Church in South Africa. Not only was the church risking the alienation and contempt of some of its white members, but it was also courting the disapproval of the apartheid government. Nevertheless, the Methodist Church's huge membership around the world and the fact that it was a Christian institution helped to undermine the philosophy advanced by apartheid leaders that the Christian church approved of policies of segregation. A cry for fundamental political change was being made, not by individuals who could be accused of being communists and violent agitators, but by an entire Christian organization that claimed to speak on behalf of God. The government might have been able to control Afrikaans churches, but they were unable to change the religious views of members of the South African Council of Churches.

In 1987, Reverend Scholtz and Dr. Stanley Mogoba, a former Robben Island prisoner who would become presiding bishop of the Methodist Church the following year, travelled to Lusaka, the home of the exiled ANC and other liberation movements at the time, to attend a consultation of the World Council of Churches titled "Programme to Combat Racism." At the conference, Scholtz and Mogoba met with Oliver Tambo and Johnson Mlambo, presidents of the ANC and PAC respectively. These two prominent struggle leaders were at the conference not just to talk about apartheid, but also to meet African theologians who could assist them in opposing it.

Scholtz's desire to speak out against apartheid was informed by his childhood experiences in Bloemfontein, when he had witnessed how badly black people in the area were treated by the ruling white establishment. In May 1977, when Winnie Mandela and her daughter Zindzi were forcibly removed from their Soweto home and banished to the Free State town of Brandfort, Scholtz, who at the time was the chairman (today he would be called the bishop) of the district of the Free State, had regarded it as his duty to minister to Winnie as a show of gratitude for her contribution to the struggle.[33] When he became president of the Methodist Church in 1986, Scholtz realized that Mandela had not been visited by a single prominent leader of the Methodist Church since his imprisonment, so he wrote to the Department of Justice and requested permission to visit the activist and to minister to him.

Prison authorities were hesitant at first, but John Scholtz was not the kind of person to be denied and he wrote back to the prison, reminding the people in charge that the Methodist Church had five million members in South Africa, and if news got out that the head of the church had not been permitted to visit Mandela, it would not be well received. Scholtz's request was forwarded to the minister of justice, Kobie Coetsee, who suspected that the bishop was trying to generate political mileage by visiting Mandela in prison. But after meeting with Coetsee in Cape Town, Scholtz was able to convince him that his only intention in calling on Mandela was to show him support and to give him spiritual guidance. "My response was that.... It would be a pastoral visit but that I would affirm and encourage Mr. Mandela in the justice of his cause and remind him that there were many who stood with him in his vision for a free South Africa," Scholtz later wrote.[34] Coetsee sanctioned Scholtz's visit to Mandela, but with the proviso that the meeting be supervised by the chaplain general of the South African Prison Services.

Scholtz describes his first visit with Mandela in 1987 as "absolutely wonderful." After being led into a noisy committee room in the prison, Scholtz waited for the political activist, whose height surprised him when he first saw him. To Scholtz, Mandela said, "Mr. President, good morning. Thank you so much for looking after my wife in Brandfort." Scholtz replied that it was the least the Methodist Church could do for him and his family. Mandela then turned to Stanley Mogoba, who had accompanied Scholtz on the visit as his second secretary, and began to reminisce with the former Robben Island inmate about their experiences in the prison together, recalling an occasion when they had been severely punished for having a conversation in the queue at the prison's library. Mandela also cheerfully greeted the chaplain general who would be watching over the meeting: "Good morning, colonel. How are you? Are we giving you a lot of trouble?" The entire exchange astonished Scholtz: "I thought to myself, who is the prisoner here?"[35]

The men then moved on to more important topics. The Methodists informed Mandela that the call for his release was gaining momentum, before concluding their visit by giving him Holy Communion. Scholtz remembers: "I had taken the elements of Communion with me and I said to [Mandela] towards the end of our interview, 'Mr Mandela, I brought Communion elements with me, would you like for us to have Communion?' And he said: 'Oh, absolutely.'" With this response, Mandela displayed the deference that Methodists feel for the sacrament, which, according to Scholtz, is a ritual that honors "Christ in memory that he died for us, in memory of the forgiveness of sins, and acknowledge[ment of] his lordship over life."[36]

At the start of the visit, the chaplain general had seated himself at the far end of the table where Mandela's meeting with Scholtz and Mogoba was taking place. When it came time for Scholtz to give the sacrament, he moved closer to the group, and Mandela, as he had done with Christo Brand, invited the chaplain to join them. "Colonel, would you like to come and kneel with us and take Communion?" he asked. The chaplain general accepted the offer and knelt next to Mogoba. Scholtz presented Mandela with the Communion wafer before passing one over to Mogoba to serve to the chaplain general. It might even have been the first time this man had received Communion from a black hand. The entire episode greatly affected Scholtz: "It was an electric experience. It was amazing. It just [symbolized] the greatness of the man."[37]

Before bidding farewell, Scholtz presented Mandela with a small hand-carved wooden cup that he had bought in Lusaka as a gift from the people of the Methodist Church of Southern Africa. He hoped Mandela would use the cup for Holy Communion, and told him that it was a reminder of the timeless power of incarnate, reconciling love. Scholtz left the prison feeling inspired.[38]

Late in 1988, Mandela, who had been separated from his comrades in Pollsmoor and held in a different part of the facility, was quietly taken to a hospital in Cape Town's northern suburbs where he was diagnosed with tuberculosis. Seventeen weeks later, he was transported to another hospital, where he would stay until December 1988, before being surreptitiously moved to Victor Verster Prison in Paarl on the seventh day of the month. Here he stayed in his own private cottage, had a swimming pool and a cook, and could entertain visitors, including his comrades. The National Party had provided Mandela with the cottage so that his secret talks with the South African government could occur in a controlled environment without outside interference. While Mandela enjoyed the illusion of freedom that Victor Verster offered him, he "never forgot that it was a gilded cage."[39]

Regardless of the drama that perforated his political life, Mandela continued to make a point of visiting with religious ministers during his time at Victor Verster. One minister who visited him on several occasions was Methodist bishop James Gribble, to whom Dudley Moore had reported and who had also been eager to minister to Mandela. Gribble's son John was a student at the University of Cape Town, where he took a few courses with Zindzi Mandela. Whenever Gribble met with Mandela at Victor Verster, the well-being of their families was one topic they would invariably traverse. All in all, the Methodist minister and the political prisoner were very comfortable with each other. "We chatted on first name terms," Gribble says. "I was James, he was Nelson."[40]

As with other ministers, Gribble and Mandela's meetings were underscored by moments of deep spiritual meditation, especially around Holy Communion. Gribble remembers that Mandela happily received the sacrament. The minister for his part was honored to share with Mandela this act of thanksgiving, which he regards as the "deepest form of Christian fellowship."[41]

Gribble came away from these encounters with Mandela feeling "blessed" at having been able to witness the icon's "regal bearing." "There was dignity about him," Gribble remembers, "a depth and an absolute absence of bitterness or rancor. I just found that astonishing after what had been done to him."[42]

The last time Gribble saw Mandela was on September, 14 1989. They sat down together to a lunch prepared by Mandela's warder, and discussed church and political events. Mandela also shared with Gribble his concerns for Winnie, whose involvement in the abduction of four boys from a Methodist manse in Orlando West in December 1988, resulting in the murder of one of the youths, Stompie Seipei, had been publicly condemned by the Mass Democratic Movement in February. Mandela told Gribble that he felt helpless, unable to do anything about it because he was in prison.

Through his ability to listen to and accept many points of view, and his deep and unshakable faith, Mandela proved to the religious leaders he encountered during his prison years that he was capable of being a strong and inspirational leader, even behind bars. Mandela was indeed a natural leader who could command loyalty and respect from the most unlikely people. But he was equally able to show loyalty and respect, especially to those who served him or the anti-apartheid struggle. He never forgot the courage shown by the likes of Harry Wiggett and Dudley Moore when they chose to defend him at a time when so many people were determined to chip away at his reputation.

The spiritual lessons Mandela learned when he was ministered to by these men stayed with him even after he was released from prison. Years later, Mandela delighted a synod of Anglican bishops when he recounted how Harry Wiggett had interpreted the reason for the varying viewpoints offered by the Gospels. Using the example of four sportswriters covering a football match, Wiggett explained that each provided their own take on the match, and that none were wrong, because each writer saw the game from a different vantage point. The accounts provided in the Gospel could be interpreted in the same way, as could the perspectives of every person one encounters throughout one's life. There are many opinions and ideas that have to be heard and considered. Wiggett's analogy clearly moved Mandela, because he would reference it again at another synod, this time attended by Allan Boesak and Desmond Tutu. He said it helped him realize that, "Every viewpoint is a truth, which might not be seen or appropriated by somebody else." There was an important political truth to be learned from recognizing this fact as well. As Wiggett says, "That was a deep spiritual insight, politically; to hear what others see and yet to go forward with your own vision, but not be harnessed by it."[43]

According to Wiggett, Mandela's spirituality was a significant reason for the steadfastness and courage he showed throughout his life. Mandela's faith and trust in God guided him through the difficult times and helped him to cope with the pain of his imprisonment. "This is why," Wiggett explains, "when he went in, he was one thing; when he came out he was ripe, spiritually strong and he was whole."[44] On Robben Island, Mandela displayed great humility by listening to the opinions of someone as inexperienced as Wiggett, at that time only a junior clergyman. It was a sign of his willingness to learn more about Christian teachings.

For Wiggett, the most noteworthy feature of Mandela's faith was how he integrated his spirituality into his way of life; he not only professed to believe in the Gospel, but he also lived out its teachings, as expressed in his style of leadership and in the many kinds of relationships he cultivated. Mandela never publicly conceded that his faith influenced his political thinking because he understood how divisive the entire subject of religion could be. By openly aligning himself with one specific religious belief, Mandela knew that he would be giving the impression that he was aligned with a particular group of people, and this was not the kind of exclusivity that he sought to promote in a multiracial, post-apartheid South Africa.

Wiggett explains that this was why Mandela continued to downplay his religious beliefs even when he became president. He had gained his standing as one of the world's most iconic and well-known political leaders by promoting tolerance and equality among all people, and so did not want to appear to be endorsing any one particular ideal as president. By choosing not to identify with any one religion, he affirmed that he was an individual, and not merely a member of a group. But, Wiggett says, it was Mandela's belief in Jesus Christ that ultimately provided him with this insight.[45]

8

Confessions of Faith

THE DAY OF Nelson Mandela's release from Victor Verster Prison, Sunday, February 11, 1990, was hot with clear blue skies in the Western Cape. A large crowd of people, including a number of journalists and photographers, had been gathering outside the prison since early that morning, hoping to catch a glimpse of the man who had been imprisoned for twenty-seven years. This day would mark a change, not only in Mandela's own life, but in the mindset of the people of South Africa. Mandela would guide them towards an outlook that prioritized reconciliation and the rebuilding of a nation, after the exclusion and isolation of the old order.

Behind the scenes, others were preparing to reintroduce Mandela into society – into a world where the particulars of his daily existence would not be prescribed by prison rules and other men. This was probably a task for which many of his comrades and family members felt unprepared. How do you help a man adjust to a new life in a world that had excluded him for nearly three decades? Would he ever get used to such change? What is more: would those from whom he was separated ever become accustomed to having him back in their midst?

On the Saturday before Mandela's release, Archbishop Desmond Tutu was in Johannesburg, hosting a party at his Soweto home for the lawyers who had successfully overturned the guilty verdicts of the eleven accused in the Delmas Treason Trial. It was generally accepted that Mandela would be flown to Johannesburg and released from there. It was then expected that he would make his first public appearance in Soweto. In preparation for the event, the archbishop and his staff spent the whole of Saturday evening travelling back and forth between the Tutu residence and the Mandela home, situated on a nearby hill just a short distance away, from where the archbishop spoke to journalists who were doing live feeds of the event.

But at around four or five on Sunday morning, when the household was still asleep, the archbishop's spokesman, John Allen, was woken up by a knock on the door and informed that a private airplane, hired by the Mandela family, was waiting at Lanseria Airport to take Archbishop Tutu to Cape Town. This was where Mandela would be released. The news took Allen by surprise and he was reluctant to wake up the archbishop, who was supposed to baptize one of his grandchildren that morning. "Frankly, I did not want to present the arch with the dilemma of deserting his grandson's baptism and going to Cape Town," Allen says.[1] He therefore only informed the archbishop at half past seven that morning that Mandela would be making his first public appearance in Cape Town, when it was already too late to go with the privately hired airplane.

Tutu's staff began a frantic search for airline tickets to Cape Town for later that day, but they came up empty-handed. Fortunately, Allen and the archbishop managed to secure seats on a private jet hired by the BBC for the staff of their *Newsnight* program. When Tutu and his team arrived in Cape Town, they learned that the ANC had made a request to the Anglican Church that Mandela be allowed to stay at the archbishop's official residence in Bishopscourt on his first night as a free man.[2] The household was not sufficiently prepared for Mandela's arrival, but the kitchen was fully stocked, as Lavinia Crawford-Browne, Tutu's secretary at the time, had gone grocery shopping that day. It was decided that Lillian Noshipo Ngoboza, who was the housekeeper at Bishopscourt, would cook the archbishop's favorite dish, which she called Tutu Chicken: a curry with potatoes, green peppers and pineapples.

Crawford-Browne, in the meantime, was staffing the switchboard, taking calls from people from all over the world who wanted to know what events followed Mandela's release, where he was headed after his first appearance, and where he would hold his first press conference – questions to which Crawford-Browne did not have the answers. She had initially hoped to go to the Grand Parade, where Mandela would address the people from the balcony of City Hall, but her plans changed when she learned that she had to prepare for Madiba's arrival at Bishopscourt.[3]

(Mandela was often called Madiba. *It is the name of the clan of which Mr. Mandela was a member. A clan name is much more important than a surname, as it refers to the ancestor from which a person is descended. Madiba was the name of a Thembu chief who ruled the Transkei in the 18th century. It is considered very polite to use someone's clan name.*—Nelson Mandela Foundation)

That evening, Bishopscourt became the meeting place for a number of ANC leaders, including Walter Sisulu and his wife Albertina, Cyril Ramaphosa, Cheryl Carolus and Trevor Manuel, who were all eager to plan for the coming days. Seated in the living room with Mandela and Winnie, the group discussed Mandela's return to Soweto and the press conference that would be held the next day. After a while, Tutu entered the room and reminded the guests that they were in his house, and that he was their host for the evening. He insisted that they all pray together before continuing their discussion. Thereafter, they sang Tiyo Soga's hymn "Lizalis' idinga lakho" (Fulfill your promise).

The following day, Monday, February 12, Tutu began the morning with the Eucharist, serving Holy Communion to members of his staff and to Mandela. This, along with the fact that Mandela had stayed at the archbishop's residence on the first night of his release, were powerful indicators of the esteem in which Tutu was held by Mandela.

It had been decided that Mandela's first press conference would also be held at Bishopscourt, and that ANC activist Cheryl Carolus would accompany him and Winnie to a photo session beforehand, where they would be photographed with Walter and Albertina Sisulu. Archbishop Tutu was apparently very excited by the entire affair, eagerly leading the group, who followed him at a more dignified pace, down the steps into his garden where the photoshoot and subsequent press conference were to be held. During the shoot, Mandela's face often appeared frozen and the photographers tried to get him to look more animated. But his eyes had sustained permanent damage from their constant exposure to the sun's glare when he worked in the lime quarry on Robben Island, and he was sensitive to camera flashes. So Tutu, remembers Allen, attempted to get Mandela to relax by joking with him, "Hey man, you have a wonderful smile. You must smile for the press more often. You must smile, man." When it was time for the actual press conference, however, the archbishop, understanding that this was Mandela's moment, quietly removed himself from the scene. A few days later, when a Danish journalist asked him about how he had helped Mandela following his release from prison, Tutu denied the significance of his role, calling himself merely an "interim leader" who retreats when it is time for the "real leaders" to do their job.[4]

John Allen, however, ascribes a substantial amount of weight to the archbishop's influence over leaders like Mandela, explaining that "he leads out and then steps back." Tutu, while he cherished the opportunity he had been given to voice his opinions and to have them taken seriously, believed that the architects of freedom, most notably Mandela, were required to take their place in the spotlight in order to express their views. It was his fervent belief in what these kinds of leaders had to offer South Africa that allowed Tutu to take a step back when they were ready and able to speak up.[5]

While Mandela stayed at Bishopscourt and got down to the business of leading millions of people to a new South Africa, Tutu spent his time making sure that the future president acclimatized to his new freedom. He arranged for his personal physician, the Swedish-born Ingrid le Roux, to examine Mandela, who immediately held out his arms to give her a hug when he saw her. Dr. le Roux remembers how pleased Mandela seemed to be at everything that was going on around him. "He was just so happy," she says, "he was radiant." She was also struck by the way that he carried himself with "great dignity, kindness, warmth and humility."[6]

Mandela, however, did not have time to truly savor the magnitude of his newfound freedom. Politics continued to consume him, to the point where his family began to feel neglected. This was perhaps not surprising given the limited contact they had had with him during his imprisonment. His daughter Zindzi spoke of the continued battle she and the rest of her family had to wage for his attention following his release from prison. "For a long time after his release there was a lot of bitterness," she said. "I never, ever imagined my father being president. I imagined him coming home and having a normal family life. When he came out of prison we only had a few moments with him as a family, before the reception committee joined us. I realized, 'He's still not mine.' I always joke that at least when he was in prison I was guaranteed two visits a month."[7] Makaziwe, his eldest daughter, also spoke of this "pain in that he was there, but not there for us."[8]

At the same time, Mandela had to adjust to life as a free man. He had become accustomed to being told where to go and what to do by other people. He now had to dispel the many myths that had built around him in the twenty-seven years he had spent in jail, as evidenced by the questions people still asked about his beliefs and his political affiliations, and even about how he looked. But the most difficult thing Mandela had to adjust to was how much the world had changed since 1962. Technological advances, for instance, completely eluded him, and his knowledge of running an office was outdated. He would need a lot of help if he was to become the leader of a free South Africa, and he got it from Barbara Masekela, a former ANC activist who was appointed his chief of staff. Her duties for Mandela involved a range of tasks, including the day-to-day management of his political campaign, and the organization of his office and home. Some were of a more personal nature, as when she had to read to Mandela the letter that Winnie had written to her lover, Dali Mpofu.

Working this closely with Mandela meant that Masekela, a member of the ANC's National Executive Committee from 1991 until 1994, got to know him as very few other people did. What she learned was that it was nearly impossible to separate the man from the politician. "I think politics was his main love. Through politics, he felt he could serve," she says. According to Masekela, Mandela believed that serving the needs of the people was the highest honor that could be afforded to anyone. For him, it was only through caring constantly for others that people could achieve their full potential.[9]

Masekela says that this was why Mandela had a number of close friends in the clergy. He respected religious leaders, and turned to them for help and advice, because he understood the importance of their role in society, which is to serve people by attending to their spiritual needs. By attempting to bring people closer to God, regardless of who or what this god means to each believer, religious leaders unite people in a common good. Mandela believed this to be a valid and worthwhile contribution to any social system, as it is only by working together that people can improve its structures. For Mandela, then, the respect that ministers received in society was completely justified.[10]

Regardless of this, Mandela continued to keep the details of his own religious beliefs private. His spirituality anchored him to the kind of morality and philosophy that underpinned the ideals he promoted throughout his lifetime, such as reconciliation and non-racialism, but he never felt the need to reveal this side of himself to the rest of the world.

Nevertheless, there were people who witnessed this hidden aspect of the president's character, such as his bodyguard, Jeremy Vearey, a former MK guerrilla who had been imprisoned on Robben Island from 1988 to 1990. Following his release from prison, Vearey worked for MK's VIP protection unit, which Mandela overhauled during the run-up to the 1994 elections, arranging for its members to receive training in modern protection methods from British security experts. Only a few of them passed, and they were honored at a graduation ceremony in Sandton that Mandela attended.

Vearey explains the uniqueness of the security personnel's dealings with Mandela: "We had a [vastly] different relationship. We were his first line of defense." They witnessed the more personal side of Mandela because of the amount of trust he placed in them, and this is how Vearey discovered just how much Mandela depended on his faith to guide him through the trials he faced every day. Vearey remembers one occasion, at a hotel in Cape Town in 1993, when he entered Mandela's room one morning to find the politician praying with a Bible next to him. Vearey was quite surprised by this scene as Mandela had never alluded to being religious or having any spiritual beliefs before this time. He quickly retreated and warned another guard not to go into the room.[11]

Vearey came to realize that this was typical of Mandela's morning routine: he would pray and study the Bible (which he also read every night, Vearey says), watch some cartoons on television and then take a walk, after which he would have breakfast. Sometimes there would be slight variations to this schedule, particularly, it seems, when Mandela was in need of more spiritual guidance than usual. On another occasion in the early 1990s, during a trip to the Western Cape, one of the guards, André Lincoln, saw a light on in Mandela's room at around three in the morning. Knocking on the door, the guard found a perfectly calm Mandela, who assured him that he had simply stayed up late praying. Perhaps the political unrest that defined this period in South Africa's history had induced Mandela to stay up late in the night to pray. Or maybe, being the spiritual man that he was, he merely found relief in engaging in the confessional elements of prayer and meditation.

Mandela's practicality regarding the training of his guards paid off in 1992 when they visited Tafelberg in the KwaZulu-Natal Midlands. There had been large-scale conflict in the area between the ANC and the Inkatha Freedom Party (IFP), who were both vying for political control of the region. Around the time Mandela chose to visit Tafelberg, an IFP *impi* (a band of Zulu fighters) had killed fifty-six people. His security advised him against traveling to the area, but he insisted on witnessing what was going on there for himself. "We drove into the area, ready to defend Madiba. He wanted to go in regardless of the risk," Vearey recalls.[12]

Mandela hoped to speak to the members of the *impi* who were causing the violence, as well as to leaders from the ANC and IFP, who had gathered together in a hall in anticipation of his arrival. In his capacity as president of the ANC, Mandela also wanted to commiserate with the locals over what they had suffered during the civil unrest, and to show them that he was not afraid to enter the conflict zone. Vearey still marvels at the composure with which Mandela handled both the meeting with the *impi* and his tour of the region to survey the chaos. Even when the violence began to escalate in Tafelberg and Vearey suggested that they retreat, Mandela responded, "No. That's why we had you guys trained. We sent you people around the world for training."[13]

This was typical of Mandela: he was able to balance his sense of duty and the idealism which underscored his political leanings with a cool knowledge of the particular pitfalls and strengths of any given situation. Years of watching Jongintaba and those he admired at Fort Hare and in the ANC had provided Mandela with a strong sense of what people required from their leaders. But it was also something within Mandela, a calmness and a sense of authority, as displayed during his interactions with his prison guards, for instance, that allowed him to peacefully navigate his dealings with others, even during times of conflict.

He maintained this equanimity throughout his day-long stay in KwaZulu-Natal, even during an excursion from Ulundi, which at one point saw him lying down in the back seat of the car as his two bodyguards, Vearey and Lincoln, attempted to get away from a vehicle that was pursuing them. They got away, and the men were again left with a sense of awe at the fearlessness their boss had exhibited during the encounter. Vearey, who was holding on to a shotgun during the ordeal, says of the experience: "The old man, let me tell you, it's amazing, I don't know how to describe it. Things happened, but he had this composure.... You hear the shots, you see the cars moving, and the old man is resolute, he wants to go in. He had confidence in us to do our job. This gave us confidence. He needed to focus on what he had to do."[14]

Barbara Masekela attributes Mandela's ability to greatly inspire the people who worked for him to his spirituality, and to his belief that circumstances could not be judged solely on appearance. Rather, Mandela understood that each person with whom he worked possessed an inner world of their own that had to be taken into account in every interaction with them. It was his spirituality that ultimately determined how he treated people and that motivated his desire to show his gratitude to all those who had supported him and the ANC during the struggle. Masekela remembers the lengths to which Mandela went, following his release from prison, to thank these individuals and organizations.[15] Included among them were the religious groups and societies that had fought against apartheid, such as the South African Council of Churches.

Founded in May 1968, during apartheid the SACC raised money for the legal fees of those who were victimized by apartheid laws, provided bursaries to poor black children, spearheaded the call for comprehensive sanctions against South Africa, and helped exiled South Africans return home after 1990 when the ANC and other organizations were unbanned. The SACC had in its ranks some of the most articulate and formidable opponents of segregation, including Desmond Tutu, Beyers Naudé and Frank Chikane. Because of its opposition to apartheid, as well as the fact that its membership was predominantly black, the SACC was deemed a "black" organization by the apartheid state in 1972.[16] In 1988, the SACC's head office in Johannesburg, Khotso House, was destroyed after a bomb, planted in its basement by the state, was detonated. The government lied and blamed the blast on MK member Shirley Gunn. A decade later, during the TRC hearings, former law and order minister Adriaan Vlok admitted that P.W. Botha had ordered the attack on Khotso House. The bombing had been carried out by the apartheid police as an act of state-sponsored terrorism. Gunn sued Vlok and others for defamation and won her case.[17]

Brigalia Bam was general secretary of the SACC from 1994 to 1999, and is no stranger to the politics of liberation. Her brother, Fikile, had been a political prisoner on Robben Island with Mandela and Sisulu from 1964 to 1975. When Brigalia Bam was executive program secretary for the Women's Department of the World Council of Churches in Geneva, she would sometimes receive messages from Mandela while he was on the island, which she would pass on to Oliver Tambo. In his messages, Mandela used the code name Holy Cross, a reference to a school of the same name that Tambo and Bam had attended together. Mandela's communications to Tambo usually included details about his situation on the island, or about the welfare of other prisoners. Bam laughs fondly when she recalls this method of communication between two of apartheid's most prominent political activists, and the role she played in facilitating it.

Mandela was deeply grateful to the SACC for its role in bringing together South African churches against apartheid. Although the SACC never officially worked with Mandela or Tambo, which would have invited a strong-arm reaction from the apartheid regime, Mandela was still thankful for the spiritual, moral and financial support the council provided to those activists who had been charged by the state under apartheid laws. During a visit to the council's chapel in East Pondoland, he communicated his gratitude and requested that the choir sing a popular Methodist hymn, "Thixo akunangqaleko, Thixo akungqibeko" (God you have no beginning, God you have no end), his mother's favorite.[18]

During his thank-you trip in March 1990, Mandela attended a memorial service at St. Anne's Catholic Church on the Cape Flats for Coline Williams and Robbie Waterwitch, two MK cadres who died when a hand grenade they were planning to plant near Athlone police station exploded prematurely. The church had attempted to keep Mandela's visit a secret so as not to draw too large a crowd to the event, but word got out, and on the morning he arrived at St. Anne's, a crowd of ANC supporters was standing outside the church waving party flags. Mandela's attendance at the church also caused controversy when he accepted Holy Communion from the Catholic archbishop of Cape Town, Lawrence Henry, during the service. The incident launched the media into a fresh debate about Mandela's religious beliefs, while the Catholic community argued whether it was appropriate for a non-Catholic to have received the sacrament in a Catholic church. Donovan Susa, an altar server at the church, had been at the rear of the crowd entering St. Anne's when Mandela arrived, and was fortunate enough to have his hand shaken by the future president. A pupil at the time, Susa recalls the hype that surrounded Mandela's visit on that Sunday. The service had to start at 9 a.m. instead of the usual 8 a.m. because of Mandela's attendance, and Archbishop Henry led the service even though St. Anne's was not his parish, thus adding to the gravity of the situation.

Susa explains that no one in the church knew if Mandela would receive Holy Communion, and were not prepared for the fallout if he did. When Mandela eventually did step forward with the rest of the congregants, Bishop Henry did not deny him the sacrament. In the aftermath, Henry's decision was questioned, even by Rome, but he countered every argument with a question of his own: was he supposed to have refused Mandela the opportunity to partake of the "body of Christ"?[19]

Mandela never commented publicly on the incident. Instead, he emphasized the importance of God, religion and spirituality in the run-up to the general election by visiting places of worship and maintaining and promoting a spiritual outlook on events among those who worked closely with him. Brigalia Bam, who was helping to run the election, and who was already awestruck by the momentousness of the occasion – in which South Africans of every race would for the first time vote together for the presidential candidate of their choosing – found herself at the end of another meaningful exchange when she received a phone call from Mandela on the day of the election, April 27, 1994.

It was six in the morning when Bam heard from Mandela, and after asking her whether she was awake (she had been up for hours), he said to her: "This is a very important day in our lives. It's an important day, but we trust you as a woman of prayer." Without waiting for her to respond, Mandela put the phone down.[20]

Bam, a civil servant, realized how significant these words were, coming from a politician of Mandela's standing. They showed that he based his trust on whether the election would be free of violence on the faith of those who were organizing it. In this moment, Bam discovered a new side of Mandela the politician. Here was someone who perceived faith and prayer as vital components for bringing success and unity to the election. After Mandela uttered those words, Bam recalls thinking to herself, "How is it that we have never thought of Mandela in this way?"[21]

Mandela's hopes that the election would take place without any incidents of violence were fulfilled. The day before his inauguration as the first black president of a democratic South Africa, Mandela stayed at Leeuwenhof in the Western Cape, the official residence of the administrator of the Cape Province, Kobus Meiring, an Africaner. Meiring, the former deputy minister of foreign affairs, had been discreetly approached by the Department of Foreign Affairs to accommodate Mandela at Leeuwenhof, as his staff wanted him to enjoy some respite from the media before the inauguration.

Meiring's wife, Bettie, made arrangements for Mandela's supper, but she was told that he would only be arriving at their house late in the evening and would eat his dinner on the airplane. Bettie, however, was adamant that Mandela would receive some sustenance in her home, and although she was told that he was unlikely to have cake, she still asked her staff to bake him a chocolate cake.

Mandela arrived at Leeuwenhof at 9 p.m. that evening. Bettie was very excited, and Kobus remembers that it felt as if "one of our favorite uncles had come to visit." Mandela seemed happy to be there, and joked about how Meiring had been the MP for Paarl when he had been moved to Victor Verster. He also had a slice of the chocolate cake, and Bettie was happy to hear that he enjoyed it.[22]

Mandela chatted with the Meirings in both Afrikaans and English, and then he had a meeting with his soon-to-be vice president, Thabo Mbeki, his minister of sport, Steve Tshwete, and Reverend Arnold Stofile, who would become the ANC chief whip in Parliament. While they talked, Meiring was on the phone until 11:30 p.m., taking messages for Mandela, including some from outgoing president F.W. de Klerk.

Before Mandela retired for the evening, Bettie asked him what time he would have breakfast the following morning. He told her that being a prisoner for twenty-seven years had made him accustomed to eating breakfast at 7 a.m. every day, so she would probably see him at that time.

The next morning, Tuesday, May 10, before Mandela appeared for breakfast, Meiring was seized with the idea to hold what he describes as a "church service" for Mandela. He turned to his son-in-law, Leon, and asked if he would sing a few hymns while he, Kobus, would say a prayer. When Mandela, looking stately in a dark suit, came down the stairs, Meiring had to brace himself. He was especially nervous about how Mandela would respond to the suggestion because, "At that stage I did not know what he believed in. You know, one had heard so many stories. For many of us in South Africa he was the devil. But I had that feeling that I must pray for him."[23]

It has been over twenty years since the occasion, and Meiring, whose first language is Afrikaans, still cannot believe how much courage he displayed when he said to Mandela, in English: "Mr. Mandela, today is probably the most important day in your life. Today you become the president of this country ... for the first time in 330 years we're going to have a democratically elected president. But ... I don't think you can do it on your own, and I certainly don't think that this country can do it on its own. Unless God is with you, it's not going to work. Would you mind before we have breakfast if I read to you from the Bible?"[24]

Mandela's response to his host was, "I will welcome that."

Meiring confessed that reading the Bible in English would not be easy for him, and so he would read from an Afrikaans Bible. He told Mandela that it had been traditional when he was in high school for the headmaster to recite Psalm 121 at assembly on the last day of school, and that he would do the same for Mandela during their makeshift church service. As a "song of ascent," it seemed especially appropriate for the occasion.

After Meiring read the psalm, Leon sang a Negro spiritual, "Brother let me be thy servant." Meiring then asked Mandela if it would be okay if he led them in prayer. He again apologized for only being able to pray in Afrikaans and not in English, but his guest assured him that he understood Afrikaans. "I want you to understand that I'm the leader of the ANC, which is an amorphous organization," Mandela said, "and its members include Jews, Muslims, Christians and people of all colors. The result is that I keep my religious beliefs private. But now I want to tell you that I grew up in the Transkei, and in those years the schools were all Christian schools. I went to a Methodist school and I'm a Christian.

Many people don't know that I was a Sunday-school teacher for four years."[25]

This confession was the last thing the Meirings were expecting. Mandela, whose personal beliefs had been the subject of intense debate while he was in prison, was regarded as the antichrist by many members of the white establishment – an enemy of the Christian faith and the religious organizations that upheld it. But with the declaration that he actually shared the religious beliefs of many of the people who considered him to be "the devil," Mandela proved, to Meiring at least, that they were "brothers in Christ."

After the prayer, Mandela had breakfast and then accepted an invitation to walk around Leeuwenhof's garden, where he met and shook hands with workers at the residence. Each time he greeted them, Mandela would say, "*Goeie môre. Hoe gaan dit? Wat is jou naam?*" (Good morning. How are you? What is your name?) Leeuwenhof's housekeeper, Retha Broderick, picked a white rose and pinned it to Mandela's lapel, and he wore the flower as he walked into Parliament later that day.

A few weeks later, the new president of South Africa sent a letter on his official letterhead to the Meiring family, thanking them in English for their hospitality. One line in the letter, written in Afrikaans, stood out: "*Baie dankie dat jy vir my huisgodsdiens gehou het en gelees het van Psalm 121.*" (Thank you very much for holding the church service for me at your home and for reading Psalm 121.)[26]

Within walking distance of the South African Parliament, in Adderley Street opposite the South African Cultural Museum, stands the Groote Kerk, home of the oldest existing congregation of the Dutch Reformed Church, the former spiritual bastion of the apartheid government, and the religious institution that sanctified the National Party's doctrine of racial segregation. For its support of apartheid, the church had been banned from membership of the World Council of Reformed Churches in 1982.[27] Now, twelve years later, it had to adjust to a society headed by the same people whose subjugation it had helped to justify.

During apartheid, it had been tradition for the head of state to be invited to the church's first service before the opening of Parliament. But now the head of state was neither an adherent of apartheid nor a member of the National Party, nor was he Afrikaans or white. Instead, he was the political activist who had been feared by the racist dispensation for decades.

But in an effort to demonstrate their willingness to be a part of the new social order in the country, the Dutch Reformed Church sent a message to Mandela's office shortly after the April 1994 election, inviting him to attend the service preceding Parliament's opening. The invite, however, was refused, and the rebuff was reported in the Afrikaans newspaper, *Die Burger*, a day before the service.

It seems that some of Mandela's staff did not understand the significance of the invitation, or of the occasion to which he was being invited. It took the head of Mandela's office, Jakes Gerwel, who had been raised in the Dutch Reformed Mission Church, to realize the implications of this decision for Mandela's reputation among members of the DRC and the white Afrikaans-speaking public. That the first black leader of South Africa was invited to a service at what had been, for decades, the most influential church in the country, was a significant occasion. It signalled the desire for reconciliation between the different races after the years of apartheid. Many Afrikaners were deeply loyal to the DRC, and it was important for the new president to prove that he acknowledged and respected their church. After reading the article in *Die Burger*, Gerwel contacted the DRC in Cape Town, informing them that despite the lateness of the RSVP, the president would definitely be at their service the next day.

When Mandela stepped into the Groote Kerk on Sunday, May 22, 1994, it certainly was a sight that many would have considered absurd or incongruous just a short time before: a former political prisoner of a racist system of government in the same church that had supported that government, and there he was, holding out an olive branch. It was a momentous event that would go a long way towards reassuring many South Africans, and not just Afrikaners, that their president was resolute in maintaining his stance of reconciliation.[28]

Mandela would go on to forge connections with various members of the DRC, even outside of strictly religious settings. In October 1996, while he was taking a walk in Houghton, he saw DRC minister Nelis Janse van Rensburg, and asked a policeman to bring the *dominee* to speak to him. Janse van Rensburg, whose congregation was based in the Northern Cape town of Postmasburg, was in Johannesburg to visit a neurologist with his wife, Aletta, and their two-year-old son, Nico, who was mentally handicapped. When Nico became restless in the doctor's consulting rooms, his father decided to take a break and went to buy a cold drink, which he drank in his car. When a policeman came up to him and told him that the president wanted to see him, Janse van Rensburg asked incredulously: "The president? Which president?"

He and the president of South Africa had a long conversation.

Mandela spoke of his sadness about the murder of DRC professor Johan Heyns, who had been assassinated in his home in Pretoria the previous year. He also spoke of his membership of the Methodist Church and told Janse van Rensburg, "Everything I know about ethics, I learned from the Methodists." Even so, he said he could not publicly declare his affiliation with the church because he was president of South Africa, and he did not want to give the impression that he was favoring one religious group over another. Despite this, he said he sought to live out his beliefs both in private and in the way he portrayed himself to the world. As in his interactions with the Meirings, it seems that Mandela, when at ease, could open up about his beliefs to people outside of the media and government – people who wanted nothing more than to speak to him for a few moments.

Before they said goodbye, Mandela put his arm around Janse van Rensburg's shoulder and suggested that they come to an agreement. "He told me he was a politician and wanted to make a deal with me: he would pray for Nico if I prayed for an important meeting he was to have the following day." Janse van Rensburg, who was named moderator, or head, of the Dutch Reformed Church in 2015, agreed.[29]

And yet, in spite of the connections he made in the DRC, and his acknowledgement of the church as a powerful religious institution, Mandela had to continually persuade church leaders, both during his presidency and afterwards, that his government needed and wanted the church's backing to obtain the trust of the Afrikaans community. The DRC leaders were unremitting in their curiosity about his religious beliefs and his views on Christianity, partly because suspicions that he was a communist still prevailed. The church might have felt entitled in their relentless interrogations of Mandela's personal beliefs, but in doing so, they helped to prove just how successful Mandela had been in creating the kind of conversational environment that encouraged debate among individuals and organizations of all types. It is debatable whether DRC leaders would have been brave enough to ask apartheid dignitaries the kinds of questions that they asked during their interrogations of Mandela, a head of state. But after years of having to defend himself against all sorts of accusations about his viewpoints, Mandela was more than prepared for the onslaught. What he would end up proving, in fact, was that he was not the person they thought he was.

Professor Pieter Potgieter, DRC moderator from 1990 to 1994, remembers one such grilling during a lunch with Mandela in Pretoria in 1993. The political violence that marred the transition to democracy had motivated Mandela and the executive of the Dutch Reformed Church to meet on several occasions to discuss threats of violent resistance that existed among far-right Afrikaners and within certain ranks of the ANC. While these meetings "took place in a good spirit and made a constructive contribution to peace in the country"[30] – an analysis based on the observations of Dr. Fritz Gaum of the DRC, who attended these meetings – there were clearly still church representatives who questioned Mandela's authority in appealing to churches for help, or discussing religious principles with them, if he was not, as they believed, a Christian. During their lunch, Potgieter confronted Mandela on this issue, asking him why he so often spoke in public about God and God's will, but never admitted to being a Christian. In response, Mandela confessed, "I believe in the Father, Son and Holy Spirit." This reply, directed to a leader of the Dutch Reformed Church, was proof of his Christian faith.

In October 2002, the question of Mandela's spiritual beliefs raised its head again during an interview at his residence in Houghton with Dr. Gaum, then editor of the DRC's *Die Kerkbode*, and Freek Swanepoel, chairman of the directors of the publication. At one point during the interview, Mandela was asked if he believed in Jesus Christ, to which he responded, "As I've said, a person's relationship with God is personal and private, but belief in Jesus is accepted by all of us."[31]

Mandela's relationship with the Dutch Reformed Church, while strained at times, greatly contributed to improving relations between white and black South Africans both prior to democracy and thereafter. In 1994, the church demonstrated its appreciation for Mandela's efforts when it invited him to speak to the General Synod of the Dutch Reformed Church in Pretoria, making him the first president of South Africa to address a DRC synod. In 2014, Reverend Freek Swanepoel, who was moderator of the church in 1994, acknowledged how much Mandela had contributed to reconciliation politics in South Africa when he sought out the DRC as an ally: "Mr. Mandela was a fine strategist who knew that the Dutch Reformed Church, being the largest of the white Afrikaans churches, had a big influence on her members. By using the church as agent for reconciliation, which is her calling, he succeeded in promoting peace in a country on the brink of civil war."[32]

In February 1999, the last year of his term in office, Mandela again visited the Groote Kerk in Adderley Street before the opening of

Parliament. During this visit, he spoke, in Afrikaans, of the first time the church had invited him to a service, and what this had meant to the burgeoning democracy of South Africa. "Without willingness of your leaders to take part in negotiations and to forgo minority rule we would never have been able to prove the prophets of doom wrong. We shouldn't allow today's doom prophets to make us miserable." He went on to thank the church for the support they had given South Africa and its government during his presidency.[33] With this expression of gratitude, Mandela once again demonstrated his belief in the ability of religion to forge relationships, no matter how unconventional.

9

A Transcendental Leader

I N SEPTEMBER 1994, almost five months after being sworn
in as president of South Africa, Mandela traveled to Mthatha
in the Transkei, where he addressed the Annual Conference of
the Methodist Church. Here, in the region where his ancestors had
laid down their roots, Mandela publicly thanked the church that
had done so much to shape his early spiritual and educational
development.

"My joy at being in this conference is multiplied many-fold by
the fact that this is for me also a personal home-coming, both in
the physical and spiritual sense," Mandela said to members of the
Methodist clergy. "The environs of Umtata are not only my humble
origins. It is here that my spiritual association with this great Church
started. And I cannot over-emphasize the role that the Methodist
Church has played in my own life."[1]

In his speech, Mandela referenced William Shaw's vision of a
chain of mission stations stretching throughout the Eastern Cape,
and how its fulfilment had resulted in the education of generations
of Xhosas, many of whom would become the country's leaders
during the struggle, and then afterwards, in a democratic South
Africa. "Although the dark night of apartheid sought to obliterate
many of these institutions, the impact of their academic and moral
teachings could not be trampled on," Mandela said. "We who passed

through them will not forget the excellent standards of teaching and the spiritual values which were imparted to us."[2]

Stanley Mogoba, president of the Methodist Church at the time, was also present at the conference. Both of these men were living embodiments of what a Methodist education had helped a number of the country's political activists to achieve.

Mandela was clearly deeply grateful to the Methodists for their sense of social responsibility towards the country's poor and denigrated. The Methodist Church acknowledged the needs of those who had been subjugated under white rule and colonialism, as well as those who had suffered under apartheid injustices. Mandela, whose political philosophy had its roots in the Christian college of Fort Hare, thanked the church for its participation in the anti-apartheid struggle and its "immense contribution to the efforts to rid our country of the scourge of racism and apartheid. When pronouncements and actions against the powers-that-be meant persecution and even death, you dared to stand up to the tyrants."[3]

During apartheid, the ruling government had deliberately targeted resistance leaders and arrested and exiled them to create a leadership void that they hoped would discourage other people from joining the uprising. But members of the Methodist clergy helped to fill this void and inspired their followers to fight against the system – ministers such as Stanley Mogoba, who had also been a political prisoner on Robben Island; Seth Mokitimi, the first black president of the Methodist Church, and who had shown Mandela at Clarkebury that black people did not have to automatically defer to white authority; Peter Storey, the reverend who had ministered to Mandela and other political prisoners on Robben Island, and who Mandela would appoint to help select the members of the Truth and Reconciliation Commission;[4] and Theo Kotze, who had spoken out fervently against apartheid before he was forced into exile, and who Mandela had described as "too political" for the apartheid government.[5]

In his address to the conference, Mandela emphasized what such activism from church organizations and their representatives had done for the struggle: "Especially while political leaders were in prison and in exile, bodies like the South African Council of Churches and its member churches resisted racial bigotry and held out a vision of a different, transformed South Africa. Methodist leaders were prominent among the prophets who refused to bow to the false god of apartheid. Your ministers also visited us in prison and cared for our families. Some of you were banned. Your Presiding Bishop [Mogoba] himself shared imprisonment with us for some years on Robben Island. This you did, not as outsiders to the cause of democracy, but as part of society and eminent prophets of the teachings of your faith."[6]

Mandela never forgot the Methodist Church's contribution to his upbringing and his growth as a leader, and to the apartheid struggle. He wore his membership of the church as a badge of pride, and would continue to integrate what he learned from the church into his job as president of South Africa and as the patriarch of a large family. His grandson, Mandla Mandela, testifies that he also expected his family to embrace these Wesleyan teachings.

Mandla learned from his grandfather that participation in the Methodist Church was part of the legacy which he and the rest of Mandela's children and grandchildren had inherited from him. Due to Mandela's imprisonment for much of his childhood, Mandla had been raised in the Catholic Church. It would be some time before he learned about his rich family history and his famous grandfather, never mind his Methodist heritage.

"My mother [Rennie Mandela-Perry] tells me that the first incident when I met my grandfather was when I was two months old," Mandla says. "She had actually put me in her bag going to Robben Island. She was fortunate to go through all the security checks without them picking up that she was carrying me in there. I was fast asleep. By the time she was … with my father [Mandela's son Makgatho] and my grandfather, she pulled me out of the bag and said, 'I'd like to present your grandchild to you.'"[7] The visit was naturally a very emotional one for Mandela.

Mandla would only see his grandfather again in 1983 when he was nine years old, when Mandela was in Pollsmoor Prison. At the time, Mandla was living in Soweto, in the midst of the student protests that were sweeping South Africa, and he could not help but hear the ubiquitous cry of "*Amandla*" (power) reverberating in the township. Mandla recalls his mistaken belief that the protesters were calling out his name. "I would think I was very popular," he says. His sense of his own importance only increased when he heard the crowds shouting, "Viva, Mandela! Viva!"

"My name, my surname," Mandla notes. "I thought I must be a most important person. So I'd run home with my fists in the air, going to my father and saying, 'I'm well known out there. Everyone is screaming my name.' My father would laugh, break down in stitches. 'Ah I've got an idiot of a child.' So he put me on this journey of self-discovery, arranged with his younger sister, Zindzi."[8]

Zindzi took her nephew to Brandfort in her Volkswagen Beetle to meet Winnie Mandela, his grandfather's second wife. When they arrived in the early evening, Mandla was surprised to see a very excited woman running out of her house to greet him. "Where's my grandson?" she called out. "Where is this child? Bring him out of the car."

Mandla was astonished to learn that this woman calling herself his grandmother was "Mum Winnie." He was confused, too. "I was meeting her for the first time, introducing herself as my grandmother. I was very puzzled, because growing up, I knew my grandmothers to be Anna Mosehla, my mother's mother, and also Evelyn on the paternal side, my father's mother. It was a very strange moment for me. She kept me up almost the whole evening and we must have gone to sleep about midnight. She was telling me different stories of who she is."[9]

During the journey to visit his grandfather, Mandla flew on an airplane for the first time in his life. The flight was difficult – there was a lot of turbulence and he remembers his ears being blocked for much of the trip. When he arrived in Cape Town, he recalls the cultural shock of seeing two people of a different race waiting for him and Winnie at the airport. They were Dullah and Farida Omar.

The Omars took Mandla and Winnie to see Mandela at Pollsmoor, and Mandla is still deeply grateful to the couple for introducing him to his famous grandparent. "If you ask Aunt Farida particularly who had introduced the young Mandla to the old man, they'll say it was us. Farida still cries every time I tell her if there are people to thank for introducing me to this global icon, to this founding father of our young democracy, it was absolutely Dullah and Farida Omar."[10]

The nervous nine-year-old sat with Winnie in the prison's waiting room, where he marveled at the size and security of the building. "Every window has got bars. Every door has got bars." As the full realization of where he was hit him, Mandla retreated into himself. Everything he had ever learned about prison had emphasized that it was a place that housed the worst people in society. He started to question the character of the man he was visiting, and found himself becoming angry, too, at this person who had "shamed our family."

He suddenly heard the deep, booming voice of a man walking down the corridor. It was Mandela, who was making polite conversation with the guards, inquiring after their health and their families. This already indicated what kind of person Mandela was, but Mandla, as a child who had learned very little about his grandfather, could not see this.

When Mandela finally entered the waiting room, Mandla was awed. "A giant came into the room. My grandfather was built of a bigger stature than myself. He was six foot five at his peak, taller than I am now." Winnie jumped up and ran to hug her husband, crying and thrilled to see him. But Mandla sat still and said nothing. Eventually, Mandela looked at him and said, "Oh you must be my grandson." Upon hearing this greeting, Mandla felt his bitterness increase.[11]

Conversation between grandfather and grandson was stilted throughout the visit, the boy limiting his answers to Mandela's questions to a mere "yes" or "no." Mandla refers to the visit as the longest forty-five minutes of his life, and he was immensely relieved when it was time to go home. When he arrived back in Soweto, his father, Makgatho, asked him jokingly, "So did you find out who Mandela is?" But Mandla was too hurt and embarrassed by the experience to find the situation funny.

Mandela, however, seemed to sense what was going on in his grandson's mind. He realized that Mandla needed to be schooled in South African history and politics, so he arranged for his comrade and political activist Helen Joseph to teach his grandson about the situation in the country. In a coded letter, which went past the censors, he asked Helen to help Mandla with his English, which he feared was "very backward."

Helen invited Mandla to Norwood. It was the first time he had been in such close proximity to a white person, never mind in the home of one. Helen handed Mandela's letter over to Mandla and asked him to read it, which he did easily enough. When he was done, she said to him, "Well, even the apartheid regime couldn't understand the letter. Your grandfather says you came to visit him and you were totally clueless as to who he is and the struggle that he's committed to." She then told Mandla all about it. "And it became the irony that a white woman would educate me about who my grandfather was," Mandla muses. "These are some of the experiences I will always treasure [about] having a man like my grandfather."[12]

More lessons followed. It seemed that Mandela had set out to do for Mandla what Jongintaba had done for him: grooming and educating him so that he could become a powerful leader of the Thembu tribe.

In 1988, when Mandla was thirteen, he received one of these lessons from Oliver Tambo, who taught him about the power of appearance and the importance of looking groomed and professional at all times. Tambo was still living in London when Mandela's grandson paid him a brief visit while on his way to France to accept the Sakharov Prize on his grandfather's behalf. Mandela was receiving this award for his contribution to fighting for human rights and freedom of thought.[13] When Tambo met Mandla, the ANC president took one look at the boy, dressed in a T-shirt, denim jacket and jeans, and set off with him to Harrods, where he bought Mandla a new suit. Tambo had said to him, "You see, you are here to represent your grandfather. You must look as he did. He was a very, very clean, sharp individual."

Through such experiences, Mandla grew to appreciate who Mandela really was and what he stood for. Mandla was no longer the boy at Pollsmoor, clueless as to what his grandfather had sacrificed in the fight for freedom for his people.

Mandla continued his education directly under his grandfather when he moved into Mandela's home in Houghton after 1994. It was during this period, Mandla says, that he began to learn of his grandfather's spiritual convictions and his strong Methodist faith.

While Mandela had adhered to only one Christian doctrine for most of his life, Mandla had grown up with a mixed religious background. As a boy, he had lived with Evelyn in Cofimvaba in the Eastern Cape, where he had practiced the Jehovah's Witness faith. When he went to live with his maternal grandparents in Soweto, he converted to Catholicism, which was his religion when he moved in with Mandela. Every Sunday, he would go to the Catholic church in Rosebank. After a while, his grandfather began asking about Mandla's whereabouts. When the staff replied that Mandla was at church, Mandela would say, "He went to church? He is not out and being foolish?" And they would reassure him that Mandla was indeed at the Catholic church.

It seems their responses did little to satisfy Mandela's curiosity, and when Mandla returned home, he would be interrogated on his whereabouts on Sunday mornings. Whenever he responded that he was at the Catholic church in Rosebank, Mandela would retreat. It was clear, however, that something was bothering him, and that he was waiting for an opportunity to discuss it with his grandson.

One Sunday afternoon, he called Mandla to him and told him that they had to talk about something serious. "You know," Mandela said to his grandson, "I must inform you [that] the Mandelas … are Methodists." He went on to recount the Mandela family's history with the Methodist Church. "My great-grandfather, who was a king who ruled in 1790 to 1832, was the first in our family to commission a reverend from Grahamstown to come on a visit in 1825 to the Great Place. The reverend who visited him was Reverend William Shaw, and his visit marked the first arrival of the Methodist Church in our area as the Thembu nation. The first ever built mission station today you'll find … in Clarkebury – Mission 1300 – which is located next to the king's residence."

Mandela explained that even though his own father, Gadla, was a traditional man who had four wives, his mother, Nosekeni, was a staunch Methodist who introduced her son to Christianity. "She embraced the church in its entirety," Mandela emphasized to Mandla, "and I must point out to you that it's improper for you as a Mandela to [attend the] Roman Catholic Church." Mandela said that it was a source of pride to him that he had inherited Methodism from his mother. He still had his Methodist membership cards, he told Mandla, and he had been very active in the church before his incarceration.

Mandla remembers that whenever census representatives came to the house in Houghton and asked what the Mandelas' religious denomination was, his grandfather would proudly respond, "We are Methodists." He also had a close friend in the church, Bishop Don Dabula, whose visits he greatly enjoyed. As Mandela aged and became sick and frail, Mandla would have Bishop Dabula visit him in Qunu. When Dabula entered the house, Mandela always used to say, "Ah, Bishop Dabula, you are here. Certainly now the heavens will open for me."[14]

Dabula first met Mandela in 1962. Even then, Mandela left a great impression on him. "I saw a man who would be leader of his country," says Dabula. "The impression that he gave then was that liberation was imminent."[15] Dabula would only see Mandela again on May 19, 1989, at Victor Verster Prison, accompanied by the chief of the abaThembu, Vulindlela Mtirara, and an Anglican minister, Reverend Nompuku.

A sprightly Mandela welcomed the men and they had a long conversation over lunch, during which the priests prayed for Mandela and for the country and the government, and gave thanks for the food. "We also prayed for peace and for the abandonment of the system of apartheid," recalls Dabula, who was by now bishop of the Methodist Church in Qunu. "I was convinced he'd be released. He could be an asset to our future." After lunch, Mandela received Holy Communion from the bishop.

Dabula next saw Mandela in Soweto in 1990 when he accompanied presiding bishop Stanley Mogoba on a visit to the Mandela house. From then on, whenever Mandela went to Qunu, Dabula was there to welcome him because, "I was in charge of his spiritual welfare. Every time he came down, Graça [Machel] would phone me and tell me that the old man wanted to see me. We spent a day with him. We'd have lunch and talk."

It was one of Mandela's final wishes that Bishop Dabula officiate at his funeral, which he did in 2013. Now retired, Dabula says he

misses his long-time spiritual companion. "I was more than a chaplain: I was his friend. He loved to see me. I miss him very much."[16]

Mandla attributes his grandfather's deep emotional bond with
the Methodist Church and its ministers to the fact that he had
inherited his faith from his mother. Consequently, Methodism
was more than just a church affiliation to him. It was part of his
being and his everyday life, and he enjoyed the many aspects of
Methodist worship, which includes showing your love for God
through song. "My grandfather inherited his mother's songs and
scriptures," Mandla says. "So from time to time when we were at a
church or a song was sung that his mother used to love, he became
very emotional and he would dance to that [song] … he was moved
by song. He totally embraced choral music as hymns of the church."[17]

At the first Triennial Conference of the Methodist Church of
South Africa, held in Durban on July 17, 1998, a day before Mandela's eightieth birthday, he once again expressed his gratitude to the
Methodist Church and his mother for nourishing his spirituality
and providing him with an education:

> Today I am 79 years and 364 days old. My life has been a long
> journey. I am grateful for the learning during my early years,
> which laid the foundations for my life. I thank my mother
> and uncles who sent me to Sunday School and to the Mission
> Schools where I was nurtured. Although youth is supposed
> to rebel against a strict church, I look back fondly on the
> instruction I received at Clarkebury and Healdtown. The
> values I was taught at these institutions have served me well
> throughout my life. These values were strengthened during
> our years of incarceration when this church, along with other

religious communities, cared for us. Not only did you send chaplains to encourage us, but you also assisted us materially within your means. You helped our families at a time when we could not help them ourselves. Religious organizations also played a key role in exposing apartheid for what it was – a fraud and a heresy. It was encouraging to hear of the God who did not tolerate oppression, but who stood with the oppressed.[18]

The Methodist Church had not only taught Mandela to recognize what was good and right, but also that he had to fight for these ideals. In the legacy he left to South Africa and the rest of the world, it is clear that he embraced these teachings with every aspect of his being.

In addition to Bishop Dabula, Mandela had a well-known and sometimes fraught relationship with Archbishop Desmond Tutu of the Anglican Church. Tutu, one of many youths eager to speak to the famous political activist, was in high school when he first encountered Mandela. However, Tutu never had the opportunity to visit Mandela in prison, and would only see him again in 1990, on the day of his release. When he became the archbishop of Cape Town in 1986, Tutu had wanted to visit the jailed lawyer at Pollsmoor, but he was prevented from doing so by prison authorities – even when leaders from the United Democratic Front were given permission to see him – as they feared what would happen if the fiery cleric was within conversation distance of the equally fiery Mandela.[19]

This lack of face-to-face contact between the two South African icons never took away from the mutual respect that they had for each other, both having gone to great lengths to protest the inequalities of the apartheid system. Mandela wrote letters to the archbishop from prison, but only one, mailed from Victor Verster in 1989, reached him. The letter was written on blue A4-sized paper, which Tutu asked his secretary, Lavinia Crawford-Browne, to frame for him, and which he kept in his office.

But despite their mutual esteem, it was inevitable that some of the archbishop's remarks would grate on Mandela, who could be prickly when his ego was bruised or if he felt that his motives were being questioned. In such situations, the Xhosa king in Mandela would usually reveal himself, as happened during a quarrel in 1994, probably their first since Mandela had become president.[20] During a breakfast at the president's residence in Cape Town, Tutu took it upon himself to comment on the batik silk shirts Mandela had begun wearing in public, and which many people have come to associate with him (in South Africa, this style of shirt is referred to as the "Madiba shirt"[21]). Tutu believed that it was inappropriate for someone of Mandela's stature to wear this kind of shirt to social events, especially to solemn occasions such as funerals. The archbishop suggested that the president rather wear suits because many people in South African society had "not moved that fast," and would not understand why their president dressed in this way. He also remarked that the shirts looked like pajamas. Although Tutu meant well, Mandela did not appreciate this unsolicited advice. Eventually, Tutu had to concede that Mandela could "wear his pajamas if he liked."[22]

Tutu would go on to criticize other, more serious aspects of Mandela's leadership, such as the high salaries that he approved for the ministers in his cabinet. In an address to the Diocesan Council in August 1994, three months after the ANC had won the majority of votes in South Africa's first democratic general election, the archbishop criticized the decision by government to increase ministerial salaries despite Mandela's pledge to stop the "gravy train" of rewards that the apartheid government had handed out. Tutu observed that Mandela's government "missed a golden opportunity ... to demonstrate that they were serious about stopping the gravy train.... [Instead] they stopped the gravy train only long enough to get on." In the same speech, Tutu also criticized Armscor and the arms trade: "It is appalling to know that it is South African arms which have been used in Rwanda and the Sudan. Our President could easily become the target of demonstrations and pickets and we cannot keep quiet."[23]

Mandela responded publicly to Tutu's remarks in September of that year, in a speech that highlighted his displeasure at the manner in which Tutu had aired his views. "He's a religious leader I respect very much," Mandela said of Tutu, "but he could have come to me and I would have given him the facts.... Yet he was unable to resist the temptation to jump on the bandwagon and criticize us – in many ways I consider that irresponsible."[24]

Tutu hit back at Mandela's accusation the next day. "It is very distressing that the president should behave like an ordinary politician, by not answering whether a particular argument or criticism is true, instead of impugning my integrity," Tutu retorted.[25]

It was their first public spat, something that rankled Mandela. In criticizing Tutu for not approaching him in private to voice his concerns, the president was overlooking the fact that Tutu was a representative of the Anglican Church and not of the ANC, and that his mandate came from God and not from the president. Tutu felt it was his duty as a church leader to speak out on behalf of the rest of South Africa.

Even so, disagreements between Mandela and Tutu never got so heated that they would stop speaking, or throw insults at each other. Their differences formed part of a healthy exchange of ideas and opinions between two of South Africa's most iconic freedom fighters, in a new democracy where autonomous thinking was encouraged and freedom of speech was a right rather than a privilege. In fact, Tutu observed that Mandela was "a great deal more accommodating" of criticism than other South African politicians, "who think that when you criticize them, you are condemning them root and branch."[26] Of course, angry or indignant responses to his opinions had never stopped Tutu from speaking his mind, even during apartheid, and Mandela was just the next politician following a long line of National Party politicians to be at the receiving end of Tutu's censure. The two would end up making peace over the telephone, Tutu – in typical fashion, according to John Allen – using humor to calm a tense situation and placate the disgruntled president. Making light of their feud, he said to Mandela, "Hey man, why are you attacking me?" With that, the ice between them was broken.

Mandela and Tutu's friendship formed the foundation of the healthy line of communication that they maintained throughout Mandela's term in office. The president would regularly seek out the archbishop's advice on state matters, and the latter was eager to give it. They regularly visited each other as well, and Tutu was always excited at the prospect of the long conversations he would have with Mandela on these occasions. Both men had the ability to approach different issues with humor, and neither was ever spared from being the object of the other's jokes. Allen remembers a moment at one of Tutu's birthday parties in Soweto, when the archbishop stepped forward to pleasantly remind his guests that the party had been thrown for him, and not for Nelson Mandela, who was presumably receiving the greater part of the attendees' attention. Mandela, in response, stood up and told Tutu that he was an old man who should not be partying in the first place.

After both men had retired from their respective professions, they would joke about how difficult life had become now that they had titles that were preceded by the word "former."[27]

Mandela also received spiritual counsel from the archbishop. When Tutu, in an interview with John Carlin, was asked whether Mandela had a religious and spiritual inner life, Tutu responded, "In this regard, he is a very secret person.... But I think he does have a great deal of inner resources, and that 27 years [in prison] was partly responsible." The archbishop added that Mandela had gone to church and received Holy Communion, but that he found it difficult to "invoke" this in public because it was a "very, very private" part of his life. Tutu, however, praised Mandela for keeping his religious beliefs to himself, even though "a lot of his people said that [Mandela] would have won over many others if, at that particular point, he had made some reference to God. And we should respect the fact that he refused to manipulate religion in that kind of way...."[28]

Tutu would also be a personal witness to the pain Mandela carried during his separation from Winnie, when he ministered to both of them individually. He never waited for them to approach him, but invited them to speak to him, aware that they were probably in need of spiritual guidance and consolation, especially since their separation was taking place with the whole of South Africa watching.

Tutu never spoke publicly about the break-up of the Mandela marriage while Mandela was still alive, but in 2013, in an obituary he wrote for the former president, he commented: "Soon after his release my wife, Leah, and I invited Nelson and Winnie to our Soweto home for a traditional Xhosa meal. How he adored her: all the while they were with us, he followed her every movement like a doting puppy. Later, when it was clear their marriage was in trouble, I spent some time with him. He was devastated by the breakdown of their relationship – it is no exaggeration to say that he was a broken man after their divorce, and he entered the presidency a lonely figure."[29]

Tutu therefore rejoiced for his friend when Mandela found love with Graça Machel, and was vocal in public that they should get married. Brigalia Bam indicates that Tutu had a vested interest in the relationship because of the affection he had for Mandela. "Theirs was a genuine friendship," she says, "and when Tutu felt that Mandela was not setting a good example by not marrying Graça Machel, he said Mandela must get married. He could do that in the name of friendship." Bam says the two men had a "big debate among themselves" on the matter.[30] Mandela and Graça married in 1998, with Methodist minister Mvume Dandala officiating at the ceremony.

Tutu was thrilled about the romance: "It was all the more wonderful then when he and Graca Machel, the eponymous widow of Mozambique's founding president, Samora Machel, found love together. Madiba was transformed, as excited as a teenager in love, as she restored his happiness. She was a godsend. He showed a remarkable humility when I criticized him publicly for living with her without benefit of matrimony. Some heads of state would have excoriated me. Not this one. Soon afterwards I received an invitation to his wedding."[31]

Reverend Mpho Tutu, the archbishop's daughter – who followed in her father's footsteps and became an Episcopal priest – can testify to the bond that existed between the archbishop and Nelson Mandela, having witnessed it personally. She says that what ultimately defined their relationship was a "very deep respect, really a profound respect both for the person and also for the office." Reverend Tutu explains that it was this mutual acknowledgment of each other's authority and personal outlook that allowed them to come back from a conflict as good friends, without any resentment on either side. "My sense of the tenor of Madiba's speech and conversation was that he really did have a very high regard and very profound respect for the office of the archbishop," she says. "What also did come through to me in the conversation was … a very deep respect for my father as a person, and maybe it is simply the recognition of a person of integrity, that 'I can agree with him, I can disagree with him and think that he is doing absolutely the wrong thing, but I can trust that whatever he does is in alignment with the truth as he sees and understands [it]'.… It wasn't that they were bosom buddies. There was a love."[32]

Mandela also had an affectionate relationship with Tutu's wife, Nomalizo Leah, evident in their playful banter and the way that they always teased each other. "With my mother," Reverend Tutu continues, "the relationship was slightly different. There was definitely a real fondness that was mutual." Mandela would frequently joke around with Leah Tutu almost as if she was his sister. "One of the things he would say to my mother was, 'I'm coming to your house. Make sure that you cook me a nice pot of *umngqusho* [a traditional Xhosa dish of samp, sometimes made with beans]. I'm expecting you to have cooked that *umngqusho* when I arrive.'"[33]

These kinds of exchanges were beneficial to Mandela, who as a leader was weighed down with so many responsibilities. He felt comfortable around the Tutu family, aware that he was always welcome among them and that he could turn to them for help. Reverend Tutu recalls the time Mandela was campaigning in Soweto for the 1994 election, when he visited the Tutu family, living just down the road from him, to ask for their vote. Leah was at home hanging out with her girlfriends Brigalia Bam, gender activist Joyce Piliso-Seroke and trade unionist Emma Mashinini. When Mandela entered the house, he said to the women, "I'm coming to ask you for your vote and I'll be back for the samp," which the women found very amusing.[34]

Brigalia Bam, in the work she did for both the SACC and the Independent Electoral Commission (IEC), witnessed the strong friendship that existed between Mandela and Tutu, and recalls the respect and trust that underscored their relationship. "Madiba actually very much depended on Desmond's counseling," she says. "Desmond was also one of Madiba's spiritual counselors." She remembers two occasions when Mandela, late at night, needed Tutu's help and asked Bam to get the archbishop on the phone. Bam says Tutu "was really the major person who counseled [Mandela]. ... Their friendship was genuine. Desmond would go to Madiba if he felt something was wrong, and Madiba would go to him."[35] That Mandela and Tutu shared a fervent desire to promote reconciliation in a country still marred by racial tensions was evident in their establishment of the Truth and Reconciliation Commission, a prominent and innovative political intervention for tackling and resolving racial conflict. The TRC's goal was to encourage individuals who had committed apartheid atrocities to come forward and confess their crimes, with the possibility of receiving amnesty. Through this process, the commission hoped to confront and expose some apartheid hurts as South Africa adjusted to the idea of reconciliation.

Mandela's reasoning for creating the commission was to promote unity among the different race groups of South Africa. He chose Desmond Tutu to head up the commission because, although the archbishop had spearheaded the religious aspect of the anti-apartheid struggle, he had constantly called for reconciliation between the opposing sides. His position as chairperson of the TRC would therefore bring a measure of gravitas to the process, and contribute to the strong message of forgiveness and understanding that it was advocating.

During the planning of the TRC, Mandela had many intense discussions about its organization with his minister of justice, Dullah Omar, who had also been one of his lawyers when he was a political prisoner. Brigalia Bam, still the general secretary of the SACC at this time and a member of the panel that selected the TRC commissioners, was present during some of these meetings. In their discussion about forgiveness, reconciliation and coming to terms with loss, Bam remembers a moment when Mandela said to Omar, "We are using church language here, we are using church concepts. The Truth Commission must be composed only of church members."[36]

Omar argued from a legal standpoint that church members,

while able to form part of the commission, could not be the only representatives, as the TRC had to represent South Africa in all its diversity. Although he was eventually persuaded, Mandela was saddened by this, and Bam feels that it revealed an important aspect of the former president's character: his deep respect for the church and its leaders. "I felt so bad that I'd never told the story: Mandela had said many times to me the TRC must remain a permanent program of the churches in South Africa. And, you know, I have lived with this heavy thing. He would say to me, 'This program is the church's program. It's not our program as politicians. I'm simply setting [up] the Commission to make a start and you [the churches] will continue.'"[37]

Bam emphasizes that Mandela's belief in reconciliation as an integral component of the rebuilding process in South Africa was not just an intellectual or political exercise; it seemed to come from another place deep inside him, and was something he regarded as crucial for forging connections between South Africans. "He said, 'We can't live with all the pain and their children can't live with the guilt. Our Constitution can't take people through a healing process.'"[38] This is why Mandela considered church leaders to be the perfect candidates to lead the commission, because their job was to guide people away from their pain towards a new vision.

John Scholtz believes that the terms which dictated the procedure the TRC was to follow can be found in the New Testament, "and I think that is why Desmond was asked to head it up and bring that kind of perspective – a … reconciliatory perspective. It didn't accomplish all that they wanted it to accomplish, but nevertheless it struck a note and it created, I think, a benchmark."[39]

Peter Storey, who with Brigalia Bam was on the panel that elected the TRC commissioners, attributes the spiritual foundations of Mandela's education – his years in Methodist schools and the manner in which the church welcomed him into its fold – as well as the social skills he gained from his Xhosa heritage, with informing his input in the TRC. "I have no doubt at all that the fundamental principles of grace ... which are so important in the Moravian and Methodist traditions, where there is a deep acceptance of God by everybody – where the gates ... are wide open and welcome to everyone, whoever they are, and nobody is rejected, and there's nobody excluded from the Communion table, and so it's an open table – I have no doubt that that played its part, particularly in the Healdtown years, on the formation of the magnanimity of Madiba's spirit. Just as I had no doubt that some of the best traditions of inclusion that would be part of his Xhosa culture played just as significant a role. I think his wider reading created this kind of Christian humanism, which could be a Christian-informed humanism.... He was never a formal believer in the sense of all the doctrinal jots and tittles, but the spirit of Jesus and his welcoming spirit, I think, were profoundly central to his own character."[40]

Storey also indicates that Mandela's attitude post-apartheid, which emphasized reconciliation, forgiveness and tolerance, led him to using the TRC as a means of confronting past wrongs. "He just had to be who he was to make the TRC logical under the circumstances, I think. You know, if somebody of a much more unforgiving spirit had come into leadership, the TRC – I doubt it would have got off the ground. So he created the ethos in which ... it could blossom." Storey believes that the TRC was the best way for South Africans to confront their history. "I have no hesitation at all to say that that was the right way to go. We may have ended that process too early.... I don't think we were as thorough as we could have been, but there's nothing wrong with the process. I think it was inspired."[41]

At the end of the day, and perhaps inevitably, a number of people were unhappy with the outcome. After the TRC hearings, there were many who felt that their loved ones and family members who had been wronged during apartheid were not given the justice they deserved.

Methodist reverend Vukile Mehana, who at Mandela's recommendation had been the first post-exile chaplain general of the ANC from 1997 to 2014, describes Mandela as a "transcendental leader, a leader who is informed by spirituality. He didn't seek to do good because it was the politically right thing to do." Instead, Reverend Mehana says, Mandela promoted reconciliation and forgiveness because he considered it to be his duty – a duty that was bestowed on him by God. The empathy Mandela shared with those who had suffered past wrongs, and with the poor and displaced, informed his leadership of the country. As a servant of God, he fervently believed that he existed to serve these people. The reverend explains the philosophy that underpinned this conviction: "Mandela's attitude was: if there's any crumb left, I'm worthy of it – after everybody else."[42] As the foremost representative of South Africa's people, Mandela accepted the fact that his needs came second to theirs, especially after everything they had suffered. In his formation of the Truth and Reconciliation Commission to address past wrongs, he was merely fulfilling his duty as an agent of God's will.

10

Last Rites

M ANDELA SERVED AS president of South Africa for one term. Following his retirement as president in 1999, Thabo Mbeki became the country's new leader. The latter had been raised at the center of the ANC's resistance campaign, receiving his political education from ANC stalwarts such as Govan Mbeki, his father, as well as from the leader of the party, Oliver Tambo. Predictably, he never acquired the same amount of veneration that Mandela had received. And while a brilliant man, some South Africans considered Mbeki to be an aloof figure, indifferent to their needs, and not as driven by reconciliation as Mandela had been.

Desmond Tutu witnessed first-hand the changed philosophy that came with the country's new leadership, finding the open door that had always welcomed him into Mandela's office for counsel and discussion now shut tight by the group of former exiles who surrounded Mandela's successor. Mbeki was trying to make a name for himself outside of the South African icon's shadow, but Tutu felt slighted by his refusal to turn to him for advice as Mandela had frequently done during his presidency. As someone who had greatly contributed to the implementation of Mandela's policy of reconciliation in post-apartheid South Africa, it was difficult for Tutu to accept his limited role in Mbeki's dispensation.

But even while the figure of his predecessor continued to loom large over the period he spent in office, Mbeki could still recognize and pay due respect to what Mandela had accomplished for South Africa in the anti-apartheid struggle and thereafter. He also understood that South Africans were determined to see that these achievements never went unacknowledged or were ever forgotten by future generations. Mandela himself might not have been immortal, but the ANC had to do everything in its power to ensure that his legacy endured the test of time. One way of guaranteeing this lay in carefully coordinating the events that would follow Mandela's death, including a state funeral fit for a man of his stature, and which the world would remember for years to come. These arrangements were made in accordance with the wishes of the Mandela family and with representatives of the Methodist Church, who Mandela was determined would feature prominently in his send-off.

Bishop Ivan Abrahams, former presiding bishop of the Methodist Church and current general secretary of the World Methodist Council, claims that Mbeki was eager to start planning for Mandela's funeral immediately after he came to office, because not only would this be the first time that democratic South Africa buried a former head of state, but the entire world would be watching. It was therefore imperative that the event be planned perfectly. Included among the initial planners were Mandela's children, Makaziwe and Makgatho (who died in 2005), chaplain general of the South African National Defence Force (SANDF) Monwabisi Jamangile, ANC chaplain general Reverend Vukile Mehana, and Mandela's personal chaplain, Bishop Don Dabula. Together, they drew up a draft program for a memorial service and funeral, decided on venues for these events, and clarified the roles of the various state organs and religious bodies that would be participating. It is noteworthy that two Methodist ministers were involved in the funeral arrangements, an indication of the esteem in which Mandela held the church. Bishop Abrahams says that this is why he regarded Mandela as a father figure, because of the recognition he gave to the clergy's function in South African society.[1]

The plan for the proceedings that would follow Mandela's death was known as Project X. The state funeral aspect of the plan was quite detailed, and outlined a timetable of events over a period of ten days, from the time of Mandela's death and the president's official announcement of his passing, to the transportation of Mandela's body to the state mortuary, the coordination of daily prayer services at his home in Houghton, the memorial service, the public viewing of the body, its transport to Mthatha and the funeral service in Qunu. These plans were updated over the years.[2]

Reverend Vido Nyobole, who was general secretary of the Methodist Church from 1996 to 2006, became the coordinator of Project X in 2006. He says that Mandela was never involved in the arrangements for his funeral, but the planners knew he wished to be laid to rest in Qunu in a Methodist ceremony, and that he wanted his friend from Mount Frere, Bishop Don Dabula, to bury him. "He specifically wanted Bishop Dabula to play a prominent role [because of] the way he had related to Dabula through the years," Nyobole says. "He regarded him as his chaplain since he came from prison. Even when he was a prisoner, Bishop Dabula visited him and ... had oversight over his family, and so he regarded him as a spiritual father."[3]

Nyobole affirms that the bond that existed between Mandela and Dabula was strong: "Yes, quite a strong connection ... when Dabula appeared, you could see [Mandela's] face would beam."

It was therefore important that Nyobole, as coordinator of Project X, honor Mandela's wishes to have his good friend preside over his burial.

Even though there was an immense amount of authority and importance attached to his job as funeral coordinator, it is understandable that Nyobole did not want Mandela to die on his watch. "I was actually praying that it doesn't happen during my time in office," he says, "because ... it was a daunting task and I didn't want to take that responsibility, and so I really was hoping it would come after I was no longer there." Unfortunately, Mandela became ill and entered the last year of his life in 2013, when Nyobole was still in charge of the plan.[4]

Mandela was ninety-four years old when he was admitted to a Pretoria hospital with a lung infection on June 8, 2013. It was his third admission since December 2012, when he had been in hospital for three weeks. He remained in hospital for nearly three months – his longest stay since he had received treatment for tuberculosis in 1988, before his transfer to Victor Verster Prison. During this time, he turned ninety-five, on July 18, 2013.[5]

Mandela's hospitalization predictably attracted a huge amount of media attention in South Africa and the rest of the world. Journalists camped outside the medical facility where he was being treated throughout the time he was there, even while the South African government failed to issue regular updates on his condition to the public. President Jacob Zuma initially put an optimistic spin on the elder statesman's condition, but he later admitted that Mandela's health had worsened and that it was critical. He appealed to South Africans to keep the former president in their prayers during the period of his illness.[6] In September, Mandela returned to his Houghton home, where he received twenty-four-hour care from a team of twenty-two doctors.[7]

In all the time that Mandela was ill, and during all of the erratic events that made up his illness – the hospitalizations, discharges, and readmissions – he received a number of visits from different members of the clergy. These visitors included the president of the SACC and presiding bishop of the Methodist Church, Bishop Ziphozihle Siwa. "I visited him very often," Siwa says. "I gave Holy Communion to him and the family and to Mrs. Machel. He used to go to church. Later on, when he couldn't go, Communion was served at his home."[8]

The members of Mandela's family visited him as often as they could, congregating around him to show their love and support. Siwa is still surprised at how the branches of Mandela's immediate family – the children and grandchildren of Evelyn Mase, Winnie Mandela and Graça Machel – all came together to stand by the patriarch during his illness. On these occasions, Siwa would give them the sacrament, observing at the same time the pain that they were experiencing while they watched Mandela die: "you look at the family ... and you realize what they have been through, and so even when there [is] all sorts of media hype about their differences, personally I felt this ... family ... needed more care and ministry and compassion than most of us. But of course, being a Mandela is not easy. Your life is always public; always in the public eye."[9]

For Siwa, the greatest tragedy that the Mandela family suffered was that they never had the opportunity to fully experience the joy of having Mandela in their lives. His political career had prevented him from spending large amounts of time with them, and during his decades-long imprisonment, he had hardly had any contact with them. This might be why Siwa frequently saw them vacillate between acceptance that Mandela was going to die and hope that he might still hang on for a bit longer. This hope was no doubt encouraged by the length of Mandela's illness, which stretched out over an entire year. According to Siwa, Mandela was nevertheless aware of the fact that he had very little time left.

Mandela didn't have to face the prospect of his death by himself, however. A constant presence at his side throughout this ordeal was his third wife, Graça Machel, the woman who had breathed happiness into his life following his divorce from Winnie, when he had called himself the loneliest man in the world.[10] Siwa says that Machel basically "lived in that hospital," always showing graciousness to everyone who had been important to Mandela in his life, including Winnie, who still maintained a deep affection for her former husband even after everything they had been through.

While Siwa admits that the divorce hurt both Winnie and Mandela, particularly the latter, and that neither wanted it to happen, things turned out well in the end for the former activist when he found love with Graça Machel. When asked whether his marriage to Machel had brought Mandela happiness, Siwa responds, "Too much happiness. I think Graça was God's blessings to Mandela in the last years of his life. It was a very loving marriage." Siwa thinks this was partly because Mandela met Machel when he was leaving politics and could devote more time to his family than he had been able to do in his two previous marriages. Mandela and Machel were therefore given the chance to share many wonderful moments. "It was a beautiful marriage right until the very last day," says Siwa.

What struck Siwa most was the image of Machel sitting by Mandela's bedside with all of their children present. "It was remarkable," he says.[11]

But despite these moments of family unity, it was hard to forget why they had all come together at this time: their father and grandfather, the great Nelson Mandela, was dying. For Siwa, the entire situation was "[s]ad. Sad to see Nelson Mandela so helpless." Mandela slipped in and out of consciousness during the last phase of his illness. On the occasions when he was lucid, he received Holy Communion from Siwa or other clergymen. This, however, was not always easy to carry out because of the large number of people gathered outside the hospital. Siwa recalls the effort of having to sneak into the hospital, usually without his collar or clerical attire, which he kept in a bag until he could change in the hospital. He refused to speak to the reporters stationed outside asking him if Mandela had died yet. Siwa can attest to the fact that Mandela was indeed alive during this time, despite some people's doubts, as he "ministered to him until the very last."[12]

On the last day of Mandela's life, December 5, 2013, following a long and painful illness, it was the presence of his grandson, Mandla, by his side that helped to ease his passing. That day, Mandla, who was in Qunu at the time, had a deep conviction that he had to fly to Johannesburg to visit his grandfather.

When he entered Mandela's Houghton residence, Mandla went up to the bedroom where Mandela was lying unconscious, as he had been for weeks. Just a few moments later, Machel joined them. She came in quietly and sat in a chair near the two men, listening as Mandla talked to his grandfather.

Mandla spoke to Mandela for about an hour and a half, recalling his memories of their time together, and emphasizing how significant Mandela had been "in shaping the person that I've become. Without him, I would have never been able to achieve half of the things that I [have]," Mandla says.[13] Mandla wanted his grandfather to know that he had done everything that was necessary to make him a man capable of taking care of himself. He then began naming members of the family who had already passed, including Mandela's children, siblings and parents, and concluded with a call to Mandela to join his mother, Nosekeni, in the afterlife. "Today I release you to your mother," Mandla said to his grandfather, "for she brought you into this world. I send you back to her. That umbilical cord that was cut, let it today be joined so that the ancestors of this family can welcome you into the next life and the superior being."

When Mandla uttered these words, his grandfather started to stir, surprising Machel. She watched as Mandela nodded and tried to say something, his lips moving silently, before attempting to reach out for his grandson's hand. Mandla held onto Mandela's hand, feeling "really satisfied because I felt that I had done what I had come to do on that particular day."[14] He shares the memory of this special occasion with his Aunt Graça, who – along with the doctors present in the room at the time – was visibly moved by the exchange between the two Mandela men. Soon afterwards, her husband's organs began to fail.

Mandla had already left the house at this point, but he received a call advising him to return as his grandfather had died. Graça Machel spoke to those present at the house after Mandela's death, attributing her husband's final, peaceful goodbye to the words of his grandson, who, she said, had "released Madiba" after weeks of his being visited by so many people, including Winnie and other members of his family, and enduring so much. She added that Mandla might possess a "gift" which allowed him to do as much.[15]

Also present at the house during Mandela's passing was Reverend Vukile Mehana, who was standing in for Bishop Siwa to perform the last rites. Mehana had also visited Mandela when he was in hospital in Pretoria, during which time he and other Methodist clerics "kept close to him and the family and very quietly would go and minister to him. For us as people of the church that he belonged to, it was not for the cameras: for us it was a ministry to the family and to him," says Mehana. Throughout the time that Mandela was in a coma, those ministers were present, ready to be called on to attend to him. All of them, especially Bishop Siwa and the general secretary of the SACC, Bishop Malusi Mpumlwana of the Ethiopian Episcopal Church, were "always prepared for any eventuality," and "journeyed with the family as the Methodist Church leadership," Mehana asserts.[16]

For Mandela's last rites, Mehana held a service that was attended by the entire Mandela family. He had not prepared a sermon, he says. Instead, the reverend called on God to "speak" to him through the "written word" in order to "prepare the departure of the soul and very deeply to intercede with God to receive [Mandela's] soul." At the same time, Mehana was also there to "prepare [the family] pastorally that the hour has come." Mehana describes Mandela's passing as "so peaceful," and declares, "I know that he is resting in God's arms. I know that."[17]

Bishop Malusi Mpumlwana was also at the Mandela residence on the night of the former president's death. He was in a private room, saying a prayer from Mandela's favorite Bible verse, Numbers 6: 24–26:

> The Lord bless you
> and keep you;
> the Lord make his face shine on you
> and be gracious to you;
> the Lord turn his face toward you
> and give you peace.[18]

Bishop Mpumlwana had been reciting the verse at around 8:50 p.m. on the evening of December 5, 2013, and only found out later that Mandela had died while he was saying this prayer.[19]

Not at Mandela's bedside was his friend and personal chaplain, Bishop Don Dabula, who had been summoned by the Mandela family but was unable to get a flight to Johannesburg from the Transkei that evening.

After performing the last rites, Mehana called his colleague, Reverend Vido Nyobole, to inform him of Nelson Mandela's death, so that he could go ahead with the coordination of the funeral. President Jacob Zuma made the announcement later that night that Mandela had died, telling the world that South Africa had "lost its greatest son."[20]

Five days after Mandela's death, on December 10, 2013, an official memorial service to commemorate his life was held at FNB Stadium in Johannesburg. In addition to thousands of South Africans who traveled across the country to honor the former president, a number of foreign dignitaries and heads of state attended the ceremony, including US president Barack Obama, Brazilian president Dilma Rousseff and Indian president Pranab Mukherjee, who all gave speeches in Mandela's memory.[21]

Mandela's body lay in state for three days, from December 11 to 13. One hundred thousand people passed through the Union Buildings in Pretoria to pay homage to the former president. As demanded by Xhosa custom, Mandla Mandela sat stoically by his grandfather's side during the occasion.[22] On Saturday, December 14, 2013, Machel displayed her generosity of spirit as she stood waiting with Mandela's second wife, Winnie Madikizela-Mandela, at Waterkloof Air Force Base to hand over his body to the ANC. Both women were wearing black. Machel would wear the color for the next year, in accordance with the Xhosa mourning tradition of *ukuzila*, which requires women to cover their bodies in black and to eschew any jewellery and make-up for an established period of time following their husbands' passing.[23]

From Waterkloof, Mandela's coffin was placed on a military transport flight to Mthatha in the Eastern Cape for his burial in Qunu. When the coffin arrived in Mthatha, personnel from the army, navy and air force received it into their care. Thembu king Buyelekhaya Dalindyebo was also present at the airport to receive the body of his uncle.[24] From the airport, which had been closed to commercial flights, the funeral cortège, led by military riders on motorcycles and followed by military vehicles such as Casspir troop carriers, journeyed to Qunu, passing cheering crowds who had lined the streets to say farewell to the founding father of democratic South Africa. Over 12,000 soldiers were scattered throughout Mthatha to ensure calm.[25]

For the ANC, who had laid claim to Mandela's body and his

political legacy, the peaceful and well-planned events surrounding their former leader's farewell were a matter of honor, an attempt to prove that a black government could arrange and hold a funeral befitting the first head of state of a democratically elected government. It was also their way of acknowledging the monumental role Mandela had played as the first commander-in-chief of Umkhonto we Sizwe.

By choosing to be laid to rest in Qunu, Mandela was making a permanent return to his childhood home, where his people, the Xhosa tribe, were claiming him as their own again. They had summoned him to them after his death when they sent a small branch from an African wild olive tree, the spirit tree of the Xhosa people, to his house in Johannesburg, where a family member used it to address Mandela's spirit and persuade it to go back home to Qunu. The branch-bearer then had to travel with the branch to Qunu without speaking to anyone throughout the journey, so as to prevent Mandela's spirit from being disturbed in "its metaphysical carrying case."[26] In Qunu, Mandela's coffin, draped with the South African flag, was swathed in the skin of a lion, which is an honor Xhosa tribes reserve for those of high rank. It had previously been draped with the ANC flag, which had been handed over to a tearful Graça Machel at Waterkloof Air Force Base. A family elder remained close to the coffin to talk to the body's spirit. This tradition, known as *thetha*, allows the spirit to be aware of what is going on before its burial, because, "[w]hen the body lies there, the spirit is still alive," said Reverend Wesley Mabuza, the chairman of South Africa's Commission for the Promotion and Protection of the Rights of Cultural, Religious and Linguistic Communities.[27] On the same day, an ox was slaughtered and eaten. (Another ox would be killed a year after the funeral to signal the end of the mourning period.) Altogether, the rites and events carried out to honor Mandela in death represented "an eclectic mix of traditional rituals, Christian elements and the military honors of a state funeral."[28] They reflected the capacity Mandela had displayed in life to assimilate many viewpoints and traditions.

On the day of the funeral, December 15, 2013, a marquee accommodated the 4,500 guests who had come to pay tribute to Mandela. These included the Prince of Wales, Baptist minister and civil rights leader Jesse Jackson, Oprah Winfrey, Richard Branson, former Zambian president Kenneth Kaunda and former South African president Thabo Mbeki.

One surprise attendee at the ceremony was Mandela's good friend and political and spiritual advisor Archbishop Desmond Tutu, who had previously stated that he would not be attending the funeral because he had not been invited. As the ANC was responsible for organizing the event, many assumed that Tutu's exclusion from the list of attendees was a deliberate snub by the ruling party, although it denied the allegation. However, in the years preceding Mandela's death, Tutu had become a vocal critic of the ANC, comparing its governance of the country in 2011 to the apartheid state after it had refused the Dalai Lama a South African visa. In his criticism, Tutu had declared that "one day we will start praying for the defeat of the ANC government."[29]

According to Reverend Nyobole, Tutu was greatly offended about not being invited to his good friend's funeral, as he had hoped to play a significant part in the ceremony. A number of people spoke out against Tutu's exclusion, including Bantu Holomisa, president of the United Democratic Movement, who said,

"Mandela and Tutu were like brothers. Mandela had time for Tutu and Tutu had time for Mandela. It doesn't sound good at all." Journalist Allister Sparks emphasized that Tutu "belonged" at Mandela's funeral, explaining, "Through the period when Mandela was in jail, Tutu was effectively the leader of the liberation struggle in this country." It was only after a last-minute intervention by then minister in the presidency Trevor Manuel that the archbishop was allowed to attend. The day before the ceremony, presidential spokesperson Mac Maharaj issued a statement that Tutu would be present at the funeral. However, nobody thought of informing the funeral coordinator, so Tutu's arrival at the church came as a surprise to many as he was not listed on the program.[30]

Because of his late inclusion, Tutu had no role in the funeral ceremony itself. He was at least seated next to Reverend Nyobole, Bishop Siwa and Archbishop Thabo Makgoba, and Nyobole ensured that Tutu played a part in the burial ceremony that followed, noting that it would have been "unfair" for someone of his standing not to participate in Nelson Mandela's funeral in any way.[31]

Once all the guests were seated, Mandela's casket was carried in by senior SANDF officers, with Jacob Zuma and Mandla Mandela following behind. The coffin was laid out on a carpet of Nguni cattle skins on a podium facing the attendees, while ninety-five candles, representing each year of Mandela's life, burned behind it. Cyril Ramaphosa, the man who Mandela had hoped would succeed him as president, presided.[32]

During the ceremony, Mandela's old comrade, confidant and fellow political prisoner, Ahmed Kathrada, spoke of the road both men had traveled since they had met in 1948, and which he would now have to walk alone. Remembering his last visit to Mandela, that took place when the elderly statesman was very ill, Kathrada said, "I was filled with an overwhelming mixture of sadness, emotion and pride. He tightly held my hand until the end of my brief visit. It was profoundly heartbreaking. It brought me to the verge of tears when my thoughts automatically flashed back to the picture of the man I grew up under. How I wished I'd never had to confront the reality of what I saw."[33]

It was extremely hard for Kathrada to reconcile this image of Mandela with the strong, active man he had known on Robben Island: "What I saw at his home after his spell in hospital was this giant of a man, helpless and reduced to a shadow of his former self."

Of Mandela's death, Kathrada remarked, "And now the inevitable has happened. He has left us and is now with the 'A Team' of the ANC – the ANC in which he cut his political teeth, and the ANC for whose policy of a non-racial, non-sexist, democratic and prosperous South Africa he was prepared to die."

Kathrada had outlived all of the old stalwarts who had once made up the ANC's elite: Oliver Tambo, Walter Sisulu, and now Nelson Mandela. Talking about this loss of South Africa's greatest political activists, he said despairingly: "When Walter died, I lost a father and now I have lost a brother. My life is in a void and I don't know who to turn to."[34] His sadness seemed to reflect the feelings of many South Africans who now had to come to terms with the loss of the man they regarded as the father of their nation. The grandfatherly, humble, and kind Kathrada died on March 28, 2017. His country mourned the death of another great son.

At the request of the Mandela family, Mandela's burial was a private affair attended by only 450 guests. The burial party walked behind the gun carriage that carried the casket to the graveside, where Mandela's family stood with Archbishop Tutu, Bishop Siwa, Archbishop Makgoba, SACC secretary general Bishop Mpumlwana, ANC chaplain general Reverend Mehana, funeral coordinator Reverend Nyobole, and Mandela's good friend from the Methodist Church, Bishop Dabula. The clerics would together conduct this last part of Mandela's funeral service.

Following a military ceremony, the care of Mandela's soul was handed over to Bishops Siwa and Dabula, who did the final committal of Mandela's body to the ground. The ministers performed a typical Christian burial liturgy, including the recitation of the phrase "ashes to ashes, dust to dust" by Bishop Dabula when Mandela's soul was committed to God. This, for the bishop, was a "sad moment."[35]

Then the burial prayers were performed before the coffin was lowered into the ground, and the Mandela family was allowed to say their final goodbyes. When it was time for the tombstone to be blessed, Tutu stepped forward to honor his old friend.

That Sunday, eighty-three years after he had set out from Qunu with his mother for the Great Place, Mandela was buried on a hill in his childhood home, next to the graves of his parents and three of his children, sons Thembi and Makgatho, and his daughter Makaziwe, who had died in infancy.

For Reverend Nyobole, the finality of the occasion – the knowledge that Mandela was gone – was difficult for him to accept. "Well, it was one of those sad moments in the history of our country," he says. "Our fear was if he goes, all that he represented would go with him. That was the worst fear that we had, and indeed history is proving that."[36]

Bishop Dabula is honored that Mandela's last wish was to be buried as a Methodist. "When he was active in politics, he belonged to all, but he wanted the religious rites at his funeral to be performed by Methodist ministers," he says through tears. With this last request, Mandela had confirmed his love for the church that had nurtured his spirituality and helped to mold him into the man who would inspire millions towards a common idea of non-racialism and reconciliation.

Conclusion

DURING HIS LIFETIME, Mandela represented many things to many different people. Before anything else, he was Nelson Mandela the political activist, the man who helped bring freedom to millions of people following a long and painful struggle against racial oppression in South Africa. But there was more to him than this. To his enemies, he was a figure of evil, a terrorist, whose fervent opposition to apartheid symbolized his apparently wider hatred of Western culture and ideology, including the Christian faith that underpinned them. To his family, he was a husband and father who sacrificed the life he could have spent with them for a cause he considered to be greater than his own desires and needs, as well as theirs. And to the religious leaders who ministered to him during his decades-long imprisonment and the years after his release, Mandela was a deeply spiritual person whose devotion to his Christian faith inspired his policy of reconciliation following his election as president of post-apartheid South Africa.

Even when politics was the focal point of his existence, Mandela always acknowledged the ability of faith to unite people in a belief in a common good. When he became president of South Africa, he expressed his gratitude to the religious institutions that had spoken out against apartheid and assisted those who fought in the struggle, even when faced with persecution from the government. He also continued to maintain meaningful relationships with a number of religious leaders, including Desmond Tutu, whose close friendship with Mandela was a result of their mutual determination to liberate black South Africans from the brutality of racial segregation, and thereafter to create an atmosphere of reconciliation and tolerance in order to galvanize South Africans into working together to rebuild the country.

But even while Tutu greatly admired and respected Mandela's ability to motivate South Africans towards a shared ideal of non-racialism, he never hesitated to voice his disapproval of certain aspects of the former freedom fighter's leadership of the country. In an opinion piece written soon after Mandela's passing, Tutu spoke out about what he considered to be his friend's greatest weakness: his unwavering loyalty to his political party, the ANC. This, Tutu declared, had induced Mandela to keep incompetent ministers in his cabinet even when they should have been removed, resulting in a "tolerance of mediocrity" that "arguably laid the seeds for greater levels of mediocrity and corruptibility that were to come."[1] All that this proves, however, was that Mandela, like the rest of us, was neither without his flaws nor a model of perfection. "Was he a saint?" Tutu asked in the same article. "Not if a saint is entirely flawless. I believe he was saintly because he inspired others powerfully and revealed in his character, transparently, many of God's attributes of goodness: compassion, concern for others, desire for peace, forgiveness and reconciliation. Thank God for this remarkable gift to South Africa and the world."

Mandela's ability to bring people together was indeed a skill that few other political leaders have been able to emulate in the governance of their own countries, either in times of peace or discord. It is a talent that has been recognized by people around the world, and in a poll conducted by the BBC in 2005 to determine which of the planet's leaders its citizens would most like to head a world government, Mandela topped the list.[2]

In his own life, Mandela was able to assimilate the various beliefs, traditions and ideals that had most impacted on his viewpoint without disparaging other beliefs and traditions. He made time to observe the rites and customs of both his Christian faith and his Xhosa heritage. And while Mandela was deeply grateful to the Methodist Church for its role in bringing education to poor black South Africans, the church's current presiding bishop, Ziphozihle Siwa, criticizes the incapacity of its missionaries to show the same tolerance for African traditions in their promotion of Christianity on the continent as Mandela displayed during his presidency. "As a result, it alienated a number of people," Siwa says. "People didn't [consider] themselves part of traditional African religion. They were African people who were just religious in their own way."[3]

Mandela was aware of the dangers that came with championing one system of beliefs over another. The apartheid regime had excelled at this, and in the process diminished the dignity and belittled the values of a large number of people. Following his election as president, Mandela worked hard to reassure South Africans that their beliefs, regardless of what they were, would be defended and respected under his leadership. At his inauguration on May 10, 1994, Mandela invited religious leaders from South Africa's major denominations – including Sheikh Nazim Mohamed of the Muslim faith, Rabbi Cyril Harris from the Jewish community, Pranal Lakhani of the Hindu organization Hindu Maha Sabha, and Archbishop Desmond Tutu of the Anglican Church – to each say a prayer in acknowledgment of the momentousness of the occasion, and to demonstrate to the rest of South Africa that all religious beliefs were considered equal in this transformed, democratic society.

According to Bishop Don Dabula, Mandela's reluctance to speak publicly about his beliefs was indicative of his desire to uphold this ideal of religious equality in the new South Africa. He realized, after becoming president, that he essentially belonged to every person in South Africa, and he never wanted to give the impression that he was disconnected from anyone in any way.[4] In Reverend Vido Nyobole's opinion, this "patchwork of inclusivity" woven by Mandela allowed him to pay due respect to other religious institutions even while he treasured the role of his own church in his spiritual development and in "how he understood himself."[5]

A week after Mandela's death, at a memorial service held in his honor at Washington National Cathedral in the United States capital, Reverend Allan Boesak gave a stirring eulogy for the departed icon, in which he commanded the new generation of world leaders to follow Mandela's example and to continue to uphold the ideals that he had treasured in his lifetime. Citing the Bible as a source to which Mandela had frequently turned for spiritual counsel, Boesak indicated how the former president had used Christian scripture to maintain his devotion to ideals such as forgiveness and reconciliation, and how these ideals had ultimately found their strength in a belief in God's will and power. Boesak called on this power to continue giving its support to the fight for justice to which Mandela had devoted his life:

Let us all today now rise up again and pledge to God and pledge to all the saints of our struggle and pledge to Nelson Rolihlahla Mandela that even if it is hard, we will not stop fighting for justice. Even if it becomes difficult, we will not stop struggling for peace and we will bring good news to the poor, we will clothe the naked, we will feed the hungry, we will heal the broken-hearted, we will tell the captives that they shall be set free, we will set at liberty all the oppressed, we will fight for the dignity of all of God's children … There is so much to do in this world until all God's children can stand up and live as God's children.[6]

In his determination to unite South Africans of all races, Nelson Mandela revealed strength of character and a willingness to forgive that very few people in his position would have been able to replicate. Tutu highlighted the significance of the stance Mandela took after his release from prison when he said, "Can you imagine where South Africa would be today had [Mandela] been consumed by a lust for revenge, to want to pay back for all the humiliations and all the agony that he and his people had suffered at the hands of their white oppressors?"[7]

There were many influences in Mandela's life that helped to lead him to this path of reconciliation – his spirituality and belief in the tenets of Methodism feature prominently among them. Growing up in the church and witnessing the power that Methodist ministers exercised over the opinions of their congregants; using religion to sustain his fortitude and to continue the struggle even while in prison; and then employing religious concepts in the promotion of reconciliation in South Africa – all of this contributed to making Mandela the iconic leader we all know and admire. In the end, Mandela's spirituality had a profound effect on the legacy he left to South Africa and the world.

Notes

Introduction

1. Charles Villa-Vicencio, *The Spirit of Freedom: South African Leaders on Religion and Politics* (Berkeley: University of California Press, 1996), http://ark.cdlib.org/ark:/13030/ft4p3006kc/, last accessed July 5, 2016.
2. Natasha Marrian, "SACP confirms Nelson Mandela was a member," *Business Day*, December 6, 2013, http://www.bdlive.co.za/national/politics/2013/12/06/sacp-confirms-nelson-mandela-was-a-member, last accessed July 5, 2016; Ahmed Kathrada, personal interview, Johannesburg, February 2015.
3. Villa-Vicencio, *The Spirit of Freedom*.
4. Ibid.
5. John Carlin, "Interview: Archbishop Desmond Tutu," *PBS*, http://www.pbs.org/wgbh/pages/frontline/shows/mandela/interviews/tutu.html, last accessed July 5, 2016.
6. Villa-Vicencio, *The Spirit of Freedom*.

Chapter 1: Spiritual Origins

1. Noel Mostert, *Frontiers: The Epic of South Africa's Creation and the Creation and Tragedy of the Xhosa People* (London: Pimlico, 1993), p. 520.
2. Kevin Roy, *Zion City RSA: The Story of the Church in Southern Africa* (Cape Town: South African Baptist Historical Society, 2000).
3. Mostert, *Frontiers*, p. 597.
4. Ibid., p. 593.
5. Ibid., p. 598.
6. Ibid.
7. Martin Meredith, *Nelson Mandela: A Biography* (London: Penguin, 1997), p. 6.

8. Nelson Mandela, *Long Walk to Freedom* (Boston, New York, London: Little, Brown and Company, 1994, 1995), p. 7.
9. Ibid., p. 12.
10. Ibid., p. 13.
11. Chief Ngangomhlaba Matanzima, telephone interview, June 2015.
12. Ibid.

Chapter 2: A Methodist Education
1. Mandela, *Long Walk to Freedom*, p. 13.
2. Anthony Sampson, *Mandela: The Authorized Biography* (New York: Vintage Books, 2000), p. 9.
3. Mandela, *Long Walk to Freedom*, p. 14.
4. Sampson, *The Authorized Biography*, p. 9.
5. Mandela, *Long Walk to Freedom*, p. 15.
6. Ibid.
7. Ibid.
8. Ibid., p. 16.
9. Ibid.
10. Ibid., p. 17.
11. Ibid.
12. Ibid., p. 31.
13. Meredith, *Nelson Mandela: A Biography*, pp. 1, 12, 203.
14. Ibid., p. 13; Mandela, *Long Walk to Freedom*, p. 18.
15. Mandela, *Long Walk to Freedom*, p. 19.
16. Ibid.
17. Ibid., p. 24.
18. Ibid.
19. Sampson, *The Authorized Biography*, p. 17.
20. Mandela, *Long Walk to Freedom*, p. 32.
21. Ibid., p. 37.
22. Sampson, *The Authorized Biography*, p. 20.
23. Mandela, *Long Walk to Freedom*, p. 42.
24. Ibid., p. 38.
25. Ibid.

Chapter 3: The Runaway

1. Luli Callinicos, *Oliver Tambo: Beyond the Engeli Mountains* (Cape Town: David Philip, 2004), p. 101.
2. Mandela, *Long Walk to Freedom*, p. 47.
3. Sampson, *The Authorized Biography*, p. 15.
4. Callinicos, *Oliver Tambo,* p. 634.
5. Mandela, *Long Walk to Freedom*, p. 48.
6. Callinicos, *Oliver Tambo*, pp. 110, 111.
7. Sampson, *The Authorized Biography*, p. 26.
8. Callinicos, *Oliver Tambo*, p. 111.
9. Ibid., p. 108.
10. Fatima Meer, *Higher than Hope: The Authorized Biography of Nelson Mandela* (Johannesburg: Skotaville, 1988), p. 204.
11. Mandela, *Long Walk to Freedom*, p. 50.

Chapter 4: Politics, Before Anything Else

1. Mandela, *Long Walk to Freedom*, pp. 62, 63, 65.
2. Ibid., pp. 67, 68.
3. Sampson, *The Authorized Biography*, pp. 32, 33.
4. Meredith, *Nelson Mandela: A Biography*, p. 34.
5. See Tom Lodge, *Mandela, A Critical Life* (New York: Oxford University Press, 2006), p. 21; Sampson, *The Authorized Biography*, pp. 33, 34; Mandela, *Long Walk to Freedom*, p. 33; Meredith, *Nelson Mandela: A Biography*, p. 35.
6. Sampson, *The Authorized Biography*, p. 33.
7. Mandela, *Long Walk to Freedom*, p. 82.
8. Ibid.
9. Ibid., pp. 76, 77.
10. Meer, *Higher than Hope*, p. 31.
11. Mandela, *Long Walk to Freedom*, p. 104.
12. Meer, *Higher than Hope*, p. 32.
13. Mandela, *Long Walk to Freedom*, p. 107.
14. Ibid., p. 119.
15. "Defiance Campaign 1952," *South African History Online*, March 21, 2011, http://www.sahistory.org.za/topic/defiance-campaign-1952, last accessed July 4, 2016.

16. Ibid.; "Violence erupts during Defiance Campaign," *South African History Online*, March 16, 2011, http://www.sahistory.org.za/dated-event/violence-erupts-during-defiance-campaign, last accessed July 4, 2016.

17. Njabulo S. Ndebele, "Love and Politics: Sister Quinlan and the Future We Have," *Njabulo S. Ndebele*, December 13, 2012, http://www.njabulondebele.co.za/2012/12/love-and-politics-sister-quinlan-and-the-future-we-have-desired, last accessed July 4, 2016.

18. Adrian Hastings, *A History of African Christianity 1950–1975* (New York: Cambridge University Press, 1979), pp. 96–97.

19. Ibid., p. 97.

20. Mandela, *Long Walk to Freedom*, p. 144.

21. "The life and times of Mandela," *Nelson Rolihlahla Mandela*, http://mandela.gov.za/biography/index.html, last accessed July 14, 2016.

22. Mandela, *Long Walk to Freedom*, p. 145.

23. Meredith, *Nelson Mandela: A Biography*, p. 107.

24. Ibid., p. 108.

25. Ibid.

26. Mandela, *Long Walk to Freedom*, p. 206.

27. Ibid., pp. 206, 207.

28. "Biography of Nelson Mandela," *Nelson Mandela Foundation*, https://www.nelsonmandela.org/content/page/biography, last accessed July 22, 2016.

29. Meer, *Higher than Hope*, p. 61.

30. Ibid., pp. 62, 63.

31. Mandela, *Long Walk to Freedom*, p. 208.

Chapter 5: Taking Up Arms

1. Mandela, *Long Walk to Freedom*, pp. 214, 215.

2. Ibid., p. 215.

3. Meer, *Higher than Hope*, p. 93.

4. Ibid., p. 102.

5. Ibid., p. 107.

6. Callinicos, *Oliver Tambo*, p. 253.

7. "Resolutions of the All-In African Conference held in Pietermaritzburg," March 25–26, 1961, http://www.sahistory.org.za/archive/resolutions-all-african-conference-held-pietermaritzburg, last accessed July 4, 2016.

8. Mandela, *Long Walk to Freedom*, p. 257.
9. Meredith, *Nelson Mandela: A Biography*, p. 191.
10. Ibid., p. 265; *Conversations With Myself: Publicity Guidelines*, https://www.nelsonmandela.org/images/uploads/CWM_pub%20guidelines.pdf, last accessed July 4, 2016.
11. Mandela, *Long Walk to Freedom*, p. 270.
12. Nelson Mandela, *Conversations with Myself* (London: Macmillan, 2011), p. 76.
13. Ibid., p. 53.
14. Ibid., p. 82.
15. Frederick Quinn, "Albert John Mvumbi Luthuli," *Dictionary of African Christian Biography*, http://www.dacb.org/stories/southafrica/mvumbi_johnalbert.html, last accessed July 4, 2016.
16. Albert Luthuli, *Let My People Go* (Cape Town: Tafelberg and Houghton: Mafube Publishers, 2006), p. 232.
17. Scott Couper, *Albert Luthuli: Bound By Faith* (KwaZulu-Natal: University of KwaZulu-Natal Press, 2010), p. 157.
18. Jonathan Michie, *Reader's Guide to the Social Sciences* (New York, Routledge, 2000), p. 1003.
19. Mandela, *Conversations*, p. 52.
20. Ibid., p. 78.
21. Ibid., p. 89.
22. "December 16, the reflection of a changing South African heritage," *South African History Online*, http://www.sahistory.org.za/article/december-16-reflection-changing-south-african-heritage, last accessed July 4, 2016.
23. "Battle of Blood River," *Wikipedia*, https://en.wikipedia.org/wiki/Battle_of_Blood_River, last accessed July 4, 2016.
24. Mandela, *Long Walk to Freedom*, p. 146.

Chapter 6: An Imprisonment of the Spirit
1. Mandela, *Long Walk to Freedom*, p. 318.
2. Ibid., p. 317.
3. Anné Mariè du Preez Bezdrob, *Winnie Mandela: A Life* (Cape Town, Zebra Press, 2003), p. 115.

4. Archbishop Njongonkulu Ndungane, personal interview, Cape Town, October 2014.
5. Ibid.
6. Ibid.
7. Ibid.
8. "Makhanda (prophet)," *Wikipedia*, https://en.wikipedia.org/wiki/Makhanda_(prophet), last accessed July 5, 2016.
9. Villa-Vicencio, *The Spirit of Freedom*.
10. Ibid.
11. Ibid.
12. Ahmed Kathrada, personal interview, Johannesburg, February 2015.
13. Villa-Vicencio, *The Spirit of Freedom*.
14. Ahmed Kathrada, personal interview, Johannesburg, February 2015.
15. Bishop Peter Storey, personal interview, Cape Town, August 2014.
16. Ibid.
17. Ibid.
18. Ibid.
19. Ibid.
20. Ibid.
21. Ahmed Kathrada, personal interview, Johannesburg, February 2015.
22. Ibid.
23. Villa-Vicencio, *The Spirit of Freedom*.
24. Imam Abdurahman Bassier, *Born to Serve* (Cape Town: Boorhaanol Islam Movement, 2014), p. 122.
25. Ahmed Kathrada, personal interview, Johannesburg, February 2015.

Chapter 7: The Sacrament Behind Bars
1. Mandela, *Long Walk to Freedom*, p. 510.
2. Grey Myre, "Nelson Mandela's Adventures," *NPR*, June 2, 2013, http://www.npr.org/sections/parallels/2013/07/01/197674511/nelson-mandelas-prison-adventures, last accessed July 5, 2016.
3. Villa-Vicencio, *The Spirit of Freedom*.
4. Harry Wiggett, personal interview, Cape Town, May 2014.
5. Christo Brand, personal interview, Cape Town, February 2015.
6. Harry Wiggett, personal interview, Cape Town, May 2014.

7. Ibid.

8. Ibid.

9. "President P W Botha offers Nelson Mandela conditional release from prison," *South African History Online*, March 16, 2011, http://www. sahistory.org.za/dated-event/president-p-w-botha-offers-nelson-mandela-conditional-release-prison, last accessed July 5, 2016.

10. Fred Munro, personal interview, George, April 2015.

11. Christo Brand, personal interview, Cape Town, February 2015.

12. Fred Munro, personal interview, George, April 2015.

13. Mandela, *Long Walk to Freedom*, p. 520.

14. Ibid., p. 521.

15. "Jerry Falwell," *Wikipedia*, https://en.wikipedia.org/wiki/Jerry_Falwell, last accessed July 5, 2016.

16. Harry Wiggett, personal interview, Cape Town, May 2014.

17. Ibid.

18. David Cowell, "Police arrested prominent dissident Rev. Allan Boesak at a roadblock Tuesday," *UPI*, August 27, 1985, http://www.upi.com/ Archives/1985/08/27/Police-arrested-prominent-dissident-Rev-Allan-Boesak-at-a/7810493963200/, last accessed July 5, 2016; Times Wire Services, "South Africa police raid homes of 85 anti-apartheid activists: Leaders arrested as Cape Town riots flare again," *Los Angeles Times*, October 25, 1985, http://articles.latimes.com/1985-10-25/news/ mn-14493_1_cape-town, last accessed July 5, 2016; "Princeton group works to free clergyman in South Africa," *UPI*, August 31, 1985, http:// www.upi.com/Archives/1985/08/31/Princeton-group-works-to-free-clergyman-in-South-Africa/7572494308800/, last accessed July 5, 2016.

19. Harry Wiggett, personal interview, Cape Town, May 2014.

20. Ibid.

21. Harry Wiggett, "He shone with the light of Christ," *Church Times*, December 13, 2013, https://www.churchtimes.co.uk/articles/2013/13-december/news/world/%E2%80%98he-shone-with-the-light-of-christ%E2%80%99, last accessed July 5, 2016.

22. Harry Wiggett, personal interview, Cape Town, May 2014.

23. Ernest Moore, personal interview, Cape Town, October 2015.

24. Villa-Vicencio, *The Spirit of Freedom*.

25. Dudley Moore, "The Nelson Mandela I know: By his minister," *Weekly Mail*, September 27 to October 3, 1985, http://madiba.mg.co.za/article/1985-09-27-the-nelson-mandela-i-know-by-his-minister, last accessed July 5, 2016.

26. Ernest Moore, personal interview, Cape Town, October 2015.

27. Marrian, "SACP confirms Nelson Mandela was a member."

28. Ernest Moore, personal interview, Cape Town, October 2015.

29. "Religious Faith and Anti-Apartheid Activism," *South Africa: Overcoming Apartheid, Building Democracy*, http://overcomingapartheid.msu.edu/sidebar.php?id=65-258-6, last accessed July 5, 2016.

30. "Founding," *South African Council of Churches*, http://sacc.org.za/history/, last accessed July 5, 2016.

31. "Acts 17:26," *Bible Hub*, http://biblehub.com/acts/17-26.htm, last accessed July 5, 2016; John Scholtz, *Fire in the Bones* (Cape Town, Methodist Publishing House, 2012), p. 10.

32. Scholtz, *Fire in the Bones*, p. 10.

33. Bishop John Scholtz, personal interview, Johannesburg, July 2015.

34. Scholtz, *Fire in the Bones*, p. 111.

35. Bishop John Scholtz, personal interview, Johannesburg, July 2015.

36. Ibid.

37. Ibid.

38. Ibid.

39. Mandela, *Long Walk to Freedom*, p. 544.

40. Reverend James Gribble, personal interview, Cape Town, October 2015.

41. Ibid.

42. Ibid.

43. Harry Wiggett, personal interview, Cape Town, May 2014.

44. Ibid.

45. Ibid.

Chapter 8: Confessions of Faith

1. John Allen, personal interview, Cape Town, February 2015.

2. Ibid.

3. Lavinia Crawford-Browne, personal interview, Cape Town, June 2014.

4. John Allen, personal interview, Cape Town, February 2015.

5. Ibid.
6. Dr. Ingrid le Roux, personal interview, Cape Town, June 2014.
7. Julia Llewellyn Smith, "Zindzi Mandela interview: the father I knew," *The Telegraph*, December 15, 2013, http://www.telegraph.co.uk/news/ worldnews/nelson-mandela/10513991/Zindzi-Mandela-interview-the- father-I-knew.html, last accessed July 5, 2016.
8. Sharon Feinstein, "I watched my father die in front of my eyes … he just slipped away," *Sunday Mirror*, December 8, 2013, http:// www.sharonfeinstein.co.uk/main/interviews/Mandela_passed.php, last accessed July 5, 2016.
9. Barbara Masekela, personal interview, Johannesburg, February 2015.
10. Ibid.
11. Jeremy Vearey, personal interview, Cape Town, November 2014.
12. Ibid.
13. Ibid.
14. Ibid.
15. Barbara Masekela, personal interview, Johannesburg, February 2015.
16. "Founding," *South African Council of Churches*.
17. "Shirley Gunn," *South African History Online*, http://www.sahistory. org.za/people/shirley-gunn, last accessed July 5, 2016.
18. Brigalia Bam, personal interview, Pretoria, June 2015.
19. Donovan Susa, personal interview, Cape Town, July 2015.
20. Brigalia Bam, personal interview, Pretoria, June 2015.
21. Ibid.
22. Kobus Meiring, personal interview, Cape Town, November 2014.
23. Ibid.
24. Ibid.
25. Ibid.
26. Ibid.
27. "The Dutch Reformed Church rejoins the World Alliance of Reformed Churches," *South African History Online*, http://www.sahistory.org.za/ dated-event/dutch-reformed-church-rejoins-world-alliance-reformed- churches, last accessed July 5, 2016.
28. "Nelson beleef 'kosbare oomblikke' in Groote Kerk," *Beeld*, May 23, 1994, http://152.111.1.88/argief/berigte/beeld/1994/05/23/1/15.html, last accessed July 5, 2016.

29. Nelis Janse van Rensburg, telephone interview, June 2016.

30. Johan van der Merwe, "Between war and peace: The Dutch Reformed Church agent for peace 1990–1994," *Studia Historiae Ecclesiasticae*, vol. 40, no. 2, Pretoria, December 2014, http://www.scielo.org.za/scielo. php?script=sci_arttext&pid=S1017-04992014000300007, last accessed July 5, 2016.

31. Professor Pieter Potgieter, personal interview, Wilderness, Western Cape, June 2013.

32. Van der Merwe, "Between war and peace."

33. Address by President Nelson Mandela at a service in the Groote Kerk, Cape Town, February 7, 1999, http://www.mandela.gov.za/mandela_ speeches/1999/990207_grootekerk.htm, last accessed July 5, 2016.

Chapter 9: A Transcendental Leader

1. Address by President Nelson Mandela to the Annual Conference of the Methodist Church, September 18, 1994, http://www.mandela.gov.za/ mandela_speeches/1994/940918_methodist.htm, last accessed July 5, 2016.

2. Ibid.

3. Ibid.

4. "Peter Storey: W. Ruth and A. Morris Williams Distinguished Professor Emeritus of the Practice of Christian Ministry," *Duke Divinity School*, https://divinity.duke.edu/faculty/peter-storey, last accessed July 5, 2016.

5. Villa-Vicencio, *The Spirit of Freedom*.

6. Address by President Nelson Mandela to the Annual Conference of the Methodist Church, September 18, 1994.

7. Mandla Mandela, personal interview, Parliament, Cape Town, February 2015.

8. Ibid.

9. Ibid.

10. Ibid.

11. Ibid.

12. Ibid.

13. "Sakharov Prize," *Wikipedia*, https://en.wikipedia.org/wiki/Sakharov_ Prize, last accessed July 5, 2016.

14. Mandla Mandela, personal interview, Parliament, Cape Town, February 2015.
15. Bishop Don Dabula, telephone interview, January 2015.
16. Ibid.
17. Mandla Mandela, personal interview, Parliament, Cape Town, February 2015.
18. Address by President Nelson Mandela at the first Triennial Conference of the Methodist Church of South Africa, Durban, July 17, 1998, http://www.mandela.gov.za/mandela_speeches/1998/980717_methodist.htm, last accessed July 5, 2016.
19. John Allen, *Rabble-Rouser for Peace: The Authorized Biography of Desmond Tutu* (London: Random House, 2006), p. 281.
20. John Allen, personal interview, Cape Town, February 2015.
21. "Madiba shirt," *Wikipedia*, https://en.wikipedia.org/wiki/Madiba_shirt, last accessed July 5, 2016.
22. John Allen, personal interview, Cape Town, February 2015.
23. Desmond Tutu, *The Rainbow People of God: A Spiritual Journey from Apartheid to Freedom* (Cape Town: Double Storey, 2006), p. 264.
24. Liz Sly, "S. Africa's new leaders feel sting of criticism – Mandela, Tutu clash over big pay raises," *Chicago Tribune*, September 29, 1994.
25. Ibid.
26. John Carlin, "Interview: Archbishop Desmond Tutu."
27. John Allen, personal interview, Cape Town, February 2015.
28. John Carlin, "Interview: Archbishop Desmond Tutu."
29. "South Africa: Desmond Tutu pays tribute to Nelson Mandela," *AllAfrica*, December 5, 2013, http://allafrica.com/stories/201312051793.html, last accessed July 5, 2016.
30. Brigalia Bam, personal interview, Pretoria, June 2015.
31. "South Africa: Desmond Tutu Pays Tribute to Nelson Mandela."
32. Reverend Mpho Tutu, personal interview, Cape Town, December 2014.
33. Ibid.
34. Ibid.
35. Brigalia Bam, personal interview, Pretoria, June 2015.
36. Ibid.
37. Ibid.

38. Ibid.
39. Bishop John Scholtz, personal interview, Johannesburg, July 2015.
40. Bishop Peter Storey, personal interview, Cape Town, August 2014.
41. Ibid.
42. Reverend Vukile Mehana, personal interview, Cape Town, October 2014.

Chapter 10: Last Rites
1. Bishop Ivan Abrahams, email correspondence, October 2014.
2. Ibid.
3. Reverend Vido Nyobole, personal interview, East London, June 2015.
4. Ibid.
5. "Timeline," *Nelson Mandela Foundation*, https://www.nelsonmandela. org/content/page/timeline, last accessed July 8, 2016.
6. Khuthala Nandipha, "Zuma confirms Madiba's health improving, but still critical," *Mail & Guardian*, August 11, 2013.
7. "Mandela's health history," *Health24*, December 6, 2013, http://www. health24.com/Lifestyle/Man/Your-life/Mandelas-health-history-20130610, last accessed July 8, 2016.
8. Bishop Ziphozihle Siwa, personal interview, Johannesburg, September 2014.
9. Ibid.
10. Meredith, *Nelson Mandela: A Biography*, p. 492.
11. Bishop Ziphozihle Siwa, personal interview, Johannesburg, September 2014.
12. Ibid.
13. Mandla Mandela, personal interview, Parliament, Cape Town, February 2015.
14. Ibid.
15. Ibid.
16. Reverend Vukile Mehana, personal interview, Cape Town, October 2014.
17. Ibid.
18. "Numbers 6:24–26," *Bible Gateway*, https://www.biblegateway.com/ passage/?search=Numbers+6%3A24-26, last accessed July 8, 2016.

19. Reverend Vido Nyobole, personal interview, East London, June 2015; Reverend Vukile Mehana, personal interview, Cape Town, October 2014.
20. "Jacob Zuma addresses South Africa on Nelson Mandela's death – full text," *Guardian*, December 5, 2013, https://www.theguardian.com/world/2013/dec/05/jacob-zuma-nelson-mandela-death, last accessed July 8, 2016.
21. "Nelson Mandela memorial: Obama lauds 'giant of history,'" *BBC*, December 10, 2013, http://www.bbc.com/news/world-africa-25311513, last accessed August 2, 2016.
22. Karabo Ngoepe, Devereaux Morkel and Emsie Ferreira, "Mandela home after 9 days of mourning," *News24*, December 14, 2013, http://www.news24.com/SouthAfrica/News/Mandela-home-after-9-days-of-mourning-20131214, last accessed July 8, 2016.
23. Ngoepe, et al, "Mandela home after 9 days of mourning;" "Traditional Xhosa mourning for Graça," *DispatchLIVE*, December 10, 2013, http://www.dispatchlive.co.za/traditional-xhosa-mourning-for-graca/, last accessed July 8, 2016.
24. "King Dalindyebo receives Mandela's body despite threat to snub funeral," *City Press*, December 14, 2013, http://www.news24.com/Archives/City-Press/King-Dalindyebo-receives-Mandelas-body-despite-threat-to-snub-funeral-20150429, last accessed July 8, 2016.
25. "Lala ngoxolo, Tata Madiba!," *Department: Military Veterans*, http://www.dmv.gov.za/newsroom/gallery/nelson-mandela.htm, last accessed July 8, 2016; Greg Nicolson, "Laying Mandela to rest in Qunu – the historic day in pictures," *Daily Maverick*, December 15, 2013.
26. Daniel Howden, "Mandela funeral plans lead to tension as Xhosa leaders seek to keep traditions," *Guardian*, December 13, 2013.
27. Juergen Baetz, "Nelson Mandela's funeral included Xhosa tribal rituals," *Toronto Star*, December 15, 2013, https://www.thestar.com/news/world/2013/12/15/nelson_mandelas_funeral_included_xhosa_tribal_rituals.html, last accessed July 8, 2016.
28. Sapa, "Graca given ANC flag at ceremony," *IOL*, December 14, 2013, http://www.iol.co.za/news/south-africa/gauteng/graca-given-anc-flag-at-ceremony-1622510, last accessed July 8, 2016; "Nelson Mandela buried at Qunu ancestral home," *BBC*, December 15, 2013, http://www.bbc.com/

news/world-africa-25386729, last accessed July 8, 2016; Baetz, "Nelson Mandela's funeral included Xhosa tribal rituals."

29. Stuart Graham, "SA is now worse than apartheid state, says Tutu," *Mail & Guardian*, October 4, 2011.

30. David Smith, Daniel Howden and staff, "Desmond Tutu: I will not attend Nelson Mandela's funeral," *Guardian*, December 14, 2013, https://www.theguardian.com/world/2013/dec/14/desmond-tutu-nelson-mandela-funeral-anc, last accessed July 8, 2016; "Desmond Tutu will attend Nelson Mandela's funeral in Qunu," *Guardian*, December 14, 2013, https://www.theguardian.com/world/2013/dec/14/desmond-tutu-will-attend-nelson-mandela-funeral, last accessed July 8, 2016; Reverend Vido Nyobole, personal interview, East London, June 2015.

31. Reverend Vido Nyobole, personal interview, East London, June 2015.

32. Ed Cropley, "Madiba's journey ends at his ancestral home," *IOL*, December 15, 2013, http://www.iol.co.za/news/south-africa/madibas-journey-ends-at-his-ancestral-home-1622934, last accessed July 8, 2016.

33. "'I have lost a brother. I don't know who to turn to.' Kathrada," *eNCA*, December 15, 2013, https://www.enca.com/south-africa/i-have-lost-brother-i-dont-know-who-turn-kathrada, last accessed July 8, 2016.

34. Ibid.

35. Bishop Don Dabula, telephone interview, January 2015.

36. Reverend Vido Nyobole, personal interview, East London, June 2015.

Conclusion

1. Desmond Tutu, "Mandela was the world's most admired and most revered public figure," *Guardian*, December 8, 2013, https://www.theguardian.com/commentisfree/2013/dec/08/desmond-tutu-on-nelson-mandela, last accessed July 8, 2016.

2. "Mandela wins BBC's 'global election,'" *BBC*, September 30, 2005, http://news.bbc.co.uk/2/hi/africa/4298568.stm, last accessed July 8, 2016.

3. Bishop Ziphozihle Siwa, personal interview, Johannesburg, September 2014.

4. Bishop Don Dabula, telephone interview, January 2015.

5. Reverend Vido Nyobole, personal interview, East London, June 2015.

6. OCTDC, December 19, 2013, *Nelson Mandela Memorial Service – Washington National Cathedral, 12/11/13*, https://www.youtube.com/watch?v=7jABDU6EABA, last accessed July 8, 2016.
7. Desmond Tutu, "Mandela was the world's most admired and most revered public figure."

Bibliography

BOOKS

Allen, John. *Rabble-Rouser for Peace: The Authorized Biography of Desmond Tutu*. London: Random House, 2006.

Bassier, Abdurahman. *Born to Serve: Autobiography of Imam Abdurahman Bassier*. Cape Town: Boorhaanol Islam Movement, 2014.

Bizos, George. *Odyssey to Freedom: A Memoir by the World-Renowned Human Rights Advocate, Friend and Lawyer to Nelson Mandela*. Johannesburg: Random House, 2007.

Boraine, Alex. *What's Gone Wrong? On the Brink of a Failed State*. Johannesburg: Jonathan Ball, 2014.

Brand, Christo, and Barbara Jones. *Doing Life with Mandela: My Prisoner, My Friend*. Johannesburg: Jonathan Ball, 2014.

Callinicos, Luli. *Oliver Tambo: Beyond the Engeli Mountains*. Cape Town: David Philip, 2004.

Couper, Scott. *Albert Luthuli: Bound by Faith*. Durban: University of KwaZulu-Natal Press, 2010.

Du Preez Bezdrob, Anné Mariè. *Winnie Mandela: A Life*. Cape Town: Zebra Press, 2003.

Green, Pippa. *Choice, Not Fate: The Life and Times of Trevor Manuel*. Johannesburg: Penguin, 2008.

Hastings, Adrian. *A History of African Christianity: 1950–1975*. New York: Cambridge University Press, 1979.

Krüger, Bernhard. *The Pear Tree Blossoms: A History of the Moravian Mission Stations in South Africa, 1737–1869.* Heidelberg: Genadendal Press, 1966.

Le Grange, Zelda. *Good Morning, Mr. Mandela.* London: Penguin, 2014.

Lodge, Tom. *Mandela: A Critical Life.* New York: Oxford University Press, 2006.

Luthuli, Albert, *Let My People Go: An Autobiography.* Cape Town: Tafelberg and Houghton: Mafube Publishers, 2006.

Mandela, Nelson. *Conversations with Myself.* London: Macmillan, 2011.

———. *Long Walk to Freedom.* Boston, New York, London: Little, Brown and Company, 1994, 1995.

Meer, Fatima. *Higher than Hope: The Authorized Biography of Nelson Mandela.* Johannesburg: Skotaville, 1988.

Meredith, Martin. *Nelson Mandela: A Biography.* Middlesex: Penguin, 1997.

Michie, Jonathan. *Reader's Guide to the Social Sciences.* New York: Routledge, 2000.

Mostert, Noël. *Frontiers: The Epic of South Africa's Creation and the Creation and Tragedy of the Xhosa People.* London: Pimlico, 1993.

Odendaal, André. *The Founders: The Origins of the ANC and the Struggle for Democracy in South Africa.* Johannesburg: Jacana, 2012.

Roy, Kevin. *Zion City RSA: The Story of the Church in Southern Africa.* Cape Town: South African Baptist Historical Society, 2000.

Sampson, Anthony. *Mandela: The Authorized Biography.* New York: Vintage, 2000.

Scholtz, John. *Fire in the Bones.* Cape Town: Methodist Publishing House, 2012.

Sisulu, Elinor. *Walter & Albertina Sisulu: In Our Lifetime.* Cape Town: David Philip, 2002.

Tutu, Desmond. *The Rainbow People of God: A Spiritual Journey from Apartheid to Freedom.* Cape Town: Double Storey, 2006.

Villa-Vicencio, Charles. *The Spirit of Freedom: South African Leaders on Religion and Politics.* Berkeley: University of California Press, 1996.

ARTICLES

Baetz, Juergen. "Nelson Mandela's funeral included Xhosa tribal rituals," *Toronto Star*, December 15, 2013.

Carlin, John. "Interview: Archbishop Desmond Tutu," *PBS*. Available at http://www.pbs.org/wgbh/pages/frontline/shows/mandela/interviews/tutu.html.

Cowell, David. "Police arrested prominent dissident Rev. Allan Boesak at a roadblock Tuesday," *UPI*, August 27, 1985.

Cropley, Ed. "Madiba's journey ends at his ancestral home," *IOL*, December 15, 2013.

"Desmond Tutu will attend Nelson Mandela's funeral in Qunu," *Guardian*, December 14, 2013.

Feinstein, Sharon. "I watched my father die in front of my eyes ... he just slipped away,'" *Sunday Mirror*, December 8, 2013.

Graham, Stuart. "SA is now worse than apartheid state, says Tutu," *Mail & Guardian*, October 4, 2011.

Howden, Daniel. "Mandela funeral plans lead to tension as Xhosa leaders seek to keep traditions," *Guardian*, December 13, 2013.

"'I have lost a brother. I don't know who to turn to.' Kathrada," *eNCA*, December 15, 2013.

"Jacob Zuma addresses South Africa on Nelson Mandela's death – full text," *Guardian*, December 5, 2013.

"King Dalindyebo receives Mandela's body despite threat to snub funeral," *City Press*, December 14, 2013.

"Mandela's health history," *Health24*, December 6, 2013.

"Mandela wins BBC's 'global election,'" *BBC*, September 30, 2005.

Marrian, Natasha. "SACP confirms Nelson Mandela was a member," *Business Day*, December 6, 2013.

Moore, Dudley. "The Nelson Mandela I know: By his minister," *Weekly Mail*, September 27 to October 3, 1985.

Myre, Grey. "Nelson Mandela's Adventures," *NPR*, June 2, 2013.

Nandipha, Khuthala. "Zuma confirms Madiba's health improving, but still critical," *Mail & Guardian*, August 11, 2013.

"Nelson beleef 'kosbare oomblikke' in Groote Kerk," *Beeld*, May 23, 1994.

"Nelson Mandela buried at Qunu ancestral home," *BBC*, December 15, 2013.

"Nelson Mandela memorial: Obama lauds 'giant of history,'" *BBC*, December 10, 2013.

Ngoepe, Karabo, Devereaux Morkel and Emsie Ferreira, "Mandela home after 9 days of mourning," *News24*, December 14, 2013.

Nicolson, Greg. "Laying Mandela to rest in Qunu – the historic day in pictures," *Daily Maverick*, December 15, 2013.

"Princeton group works to free clergyman in South Africa," *UPI*, August 31, 1985.

Sapa, "Graca given ANC flag at ceremony," *IOL*, December 14, 2013.

Sly, Liz. "S. Africa's New Leaders Feel Sting Of Criticism – Mandela, Tutu Clash Over Big Pay Raises," *Chicago Tribune*, September 29, 1994.

Smith, David, Daniel Howden and staff, "Desmond Tutu: I will not attend Nelson Mandela's funeral," *Guardian*, December 14, 2013.

Smith, Julia Llewellyn. "Zindzi Mandela interview: the father I knew," *Telegraph*, December 15, 2013.

"South Africa: Desmond Tutu pays tribute to Nelson Mandela," *AllAfrica*, December 5, 2013.

Times Wire Services, "South Africa police raid homes of 85 anti-apartheid activists : Leaders arrested as Cape Town riots flare again," *Los Angeles Times*, October 25, 1985.

"Traditional Xhosa mourning for Graça," *DispatchLIVE*, December 10, 2013.

Tutu, Desmond. "Mandela was the world's most admired and most revered public figure," *Guardian*, December 8, 2013.

Van der Merwe, Johan. "Between war and peace: The Dutch Reformed Church agent for peace 1990–1994," *Studia Historiae Ecclesiasticae*, vol. 40, no. 2, Pretoria, December 2014.

Wiggett, Harry. "He shone with the light of Christ," *Church Times*, December 13, 2013.

INTERVIEWS

Ahmed Kathrada, personal interview, Johannesburg, February 2015

Barbara Masekela, personal interview, Johannesburg, February 2015

Brigalia Bam, personal interview, Pretoria, June 2015

Christo Brand, personal interview, Cape Town, February 2015

Don Dabula, telephone interview, January 2015

Donovan Susa, personal interview, Cape Town, July 2015

Ernest Moore, personal interview, Cape Town, October, 2015

Fred Munro, personal interview, George, April 2015

Harry Wiggett, personal interview, Cape Town, May 2014

Ingrid le Roux, personal interview, Cape Town, June 2014

Ivan Abrahams, email correspondence, October 2014

James Gribble, personal interview, Cape Town, October 2015

Jeremy Vearey, personal interview, Cape Town, November 2014

John Allen, personal interview, Cape Town, February 2015

John Scholtz, personal interview, Johannesburg, July 2015

Kobus Meiring, personal interview, Cape Town, November 2014

Lavinia Crawford-Browne, personal interview, Cape Town, June 2014

Mandla Mandela, personal interview, Parliament, Cape Town, February 2015

Mpho Tutu, personal interview, Cape Town, December 2014

Nelis Janse van Rensburg, telephone interview, June 2016

Ngangomhlaba Matanzima, telephone interview, June 2015

Njongonkulu Ndungane, personal interview, Cape Town, October 2014

Peter Storey, personal interview, Cape Town, August 2014

Pieter Potgieter, personal interview, Wilderness, Western Cape, June 2013

Vido Nyobole, personal interview, East London, June 2015

Vukile Mehana, personal interview, Cape Town, October 2014

Ziphozihle Siwa, personal interview, Johannesburg, September 2014

WEBSITES

Bible Gateway – https://www.biblegateway.com

Bible Hub – http://biblehub.com

Department of Military Veterans – http://www.dmv.gov.za

Dictionary of African Christian Biography – http://www.dacb.org

Duke Divinity School – https://divinity.duke.edu

Nelson Mandela Foundation – https://www.nelsonmandela.org

Nelson Rolihlahla Mandela – http://www.mandela.gov.za

Njabulo S. Ndebele – http://www.njabulondebele.co.za

South Africa: Overcoming Apartheid, Building Democracy – http://overcomingapartheid.msu.edu

South African Council of Churches – http://sacc.org.za

South African History Online – http://www.sahistory.org.za

Wikipedia – https://en.wikipedia.org

YouTube – https://www.youtube.com

Index

Abrahams, Ivan, 172–173
acceptance, Nelson Mandela's promotion
    of, 6, 48, 101–102, 107–108, 120,
    190–194
African National Congress, see ANC
African National Congress Youth League,
    see ANCYL
Alexandra, 49–50, 108
Allen, John, 124–127, 161–162
All-in African Conference, 72–74
ANC, 1–2, 48, 55–59, 69, 71–81, 115,
    125–134, 181–184
ANCYL, 55
Anglican Church, 35, 56–57, 82, 88, 100,
    108–109, 113, 124, 192
armed struggle, Nelson Mandela's support
    for, 2, 55–58, 75–78, 104–105
Armscor, 160

ballroom dancing, 37–38
Bam, Brigalia, 133–136, 163, 165–166, 168
Bam, Fikile, 88, 133
Bantu Authorities Act, 39–40
Bantu Education Act, 54
Bassier, Abdurahman, 95–97
Battle of Blood River, 78
BBC, 124, 191
Beda Hall (student hostel), 39
Bernstein, Rusty, 81
bodyguards, of Nelson Mandela,
    129–132

Boesak, Allan, 107, 113, 120, 192–193
Bokwe, Mrs., 37
Bokwe, Roseberry, 37
bombings, 78, 133
Botha, P.W., 103, 133
Brand, Christo, 101–102, 104
Branson, Richard, 183
British settlers, 10–11
British values, 22, 32
Broderick, Retha, 139
Brutus, Dennis, 36
Burger, Die, 140

Carlin, John, 162
Carolus, Cheryl, 125–126
Catholic Church, 56–57, 134–135, 149,
    154–155
cattle-killing disaster of 1856–57, 14–15
Chikane, Frank, 133
church organizations, influence on politics,
    34, 74, 112–114, 139–142, 148–149,
    189–192
circumcision, 13, 28–30
Clarke, Adam, 30
Clarkebury, 30
Coetsee, Kobie, 116
communist, beliefs that Nelson Mandela
    was, 3, 69, 103–105, 107, 110–112, 143
Couper, Scott, 76
Crawford-Browne, Lavinia, 125, 159
Crown Mines, 45–46

Dabula, Don, 4, 7, 155–157, 172–173, 180, 186–187, 192
Dalindyebo, Buyelekhaya, 181
Dalindyebo, Jongintaba, 22–27, 30–31, 42–43, 48–49
Dalindyebo, NoEngland, 27–28, 42
Dalindyebo, Nomafu, 26
Dalindyebo, Sabata, 30–31
dancing, see ballroom dancing
Dandala, Mvume, 163
Daniels, Eddie, 89
'Day of the Covenant', 78
Defiance Campaign of 1952, 55–58
De Klerk, F.W., 137
Delmas Treason Trial, 124
Dias (ferry), 95
Dickenson, Albert, 46
Diwali, 94
Dutch Reformed Church (DRC), 82, 112, 139–145

education
    Bantu Education Act, 54
    missionary, 6, 14, 16–19, 54, 147–148
election of April 27, 1994, 135–136
Ethiopian Episcopal Church, 179

Fadana, Mr., 26
Falwell, Jerry, 105–106
Ferrus, Hennie, 89
Frontier Wars, 10, 17
funeral services and burial of Nelson Mandela, 7, 156, 172–175, 180–187, 192–193

Gandhi, Mahatma, 75
Gaum, Fritz, 143–144
Gerwel, Jakes, 140–141
Giqwa, Mr., 26
Goldberg, Denis, 81, 87
Goldreich, Arthur, 81
Gqunukhwebe tribe, 14
Gribble, James, 118–119

Gribble, John, 118
Groote Kerk, 139–141, 144–145
Gunn, Shirley, 133

Hadley, Richard, 30
Harris, Cecil, 31
Harris, Cyril, 191
Healdtown (college), 31–34
Henry, Lawrence, 134–135
Heyns, Johan, 142
Hinduism, 94, 192
Hindu Maha Sabha, 192
Holomisa, Bantu, 183–184
Hughes, Alan, 88–89, 100, 109

IFP, 131
imbongi (praise-singer), 32–33, 69
Inkatha Freedom Party, see IFP
Islam, 92, 95–97, 191

Jackson, Jesse, 183
Jamangile, Monwabisi, 172–173
Janse van Rensburg, Nelis, 141–142
Japhta, Reverend, 74
Jehovah's Witness Church, 52, 59–60, 154
Jewish community, 191
Joseph, Helen, 153

Kama, brother of Chief Pato, 14
Kathrada, Ahmed, 81, 87–90, 92, 94–96, 99–100, 184–185
Kaunda, Kenneth, 183
Kerr, Alexander, 36, 41–42
Khama, Seretse, 36
Khoi people, 15
Khotso House, 133
King, Martin Luther, 104
Kotze, Theo, 149

Lakhani, Pranal, 191–192
Leeuwenhof, 136–139
Le Roux, Ingrid, 127
Let My People Go, 76

Liliesleaf Farm, 81
Lincoln, André, 130, 132
lobola (bride price), 52, 66, 69
Lofton, John, 103–107
Louw, Lionel, 107
Luthuli, Albert, 2, 56–58, 75–78
'luxuries', 37

Mabutho, J., 50–51
Mabuza, Wesley, 182
Machel, Graça, 156, 163–164, 176–179,
    181–182
Machel, Samora, 163
Madikizela, Columbus Kokani, 67–69
Madikizela-Mandela, Winnie, 65–73,
    79–80, 115–116, 119, 125–128, 150–152,
    162–163, 176, 181
Madikizela, Nomathamsanqa Gertrude,
    67–68
Maharaj, Mac, 184
Makana, Chief, 9, 86
Makgoba, Thabo, 184, 186
Mandela, Gadla Henry Mphakanyiswa
    [father], 6, 9–10, 15–19, 21–23, 67, 155
Mandela, Leaby [sister], 70
Mandela, Madiba Thembekile ('Thembi')
    [son], 53, 55, 186
Mandela, Makaziwe [daughter, born 1947],
    54, 59–60, 186
Mandela, Makaziwe [daughter, born 1954],
    60, 128, 172–173
Mandela, Makgatho [son], 54, 150, 152,
    172–173, 186
Mandela, Mandla [grandson], 4, 149–156,
    177–179, 181, 184
Mandela, Nelson Rolihlahla
    names, 21–22, 38
    family, 9–10, 15–16
    childhood, 6, 9, 16–19, 21–28
    baptism, 18, 27
    death of father, 22–23
    circumcision, 28–30
    high-school education, 30–34

at University College of Fort Hare,
    35–42
political involvement and career, 1–2,
    39, 41–42, 55–60, 65, 68–79
in Johannesburg, 43, 45–49
UNISA studies, 47, 51
at Witkin, Sidelsky and Eidelman,
    47–48, 50–51, 54–55
in Alexandra, 49–53
at University of the Witwatersrand,
    51–52, 61
meets and marries Evelyn Mase, 52–53,
    61–63, 65
children, 53, 54, 60, 66, 70–71, 72
in Orlando West, 53–54
arrests, 58, 62–63
banning order, 58–59, 68–69, 72
law firm, 61
meets and marries Winnie Madikizela,
    65–70, 79, 162–163
in hiding, 73–79
on Robben Island, 2, 79–97, 126, 150
in Pollsmoor Prison, 99–112, 115–118, 150
interview for *Washington Times*, 103–112
hospitalization of, 118
in Victor Verster Prison, 118–120, 156
release from prison, 103, 123–126
political career after imprisonment,
    127–137
as president, 136–145, 147–150
meets and marries Graça Machel,
    163–164, 176–177
retires as president, 171–172
illness and death, 174–180
funeral, 7, 156, 172–175, 180–187, 192–193
Mandela, Nonqaphi 'Fanny' Nosekeni
    [mother], 9–10, 16–18, 21–26, 40–41,
    53, 70, 155, 157–158, 178
Mandela-Perry, Rennie [daughter-in-law],
    150
Mandela, Winnie [second wife],
    see Madikizela-Mandela, Winnie
Mandela, Zenani [daughter], 70

Mandela, Zindziswa [daughter], 72, 115, 118, 127–128, 150–151

Manuel, Trevor, 125, 184

Mase, Evelyn, 52–55, 59–63, 65–66, 154

Masekela, Barbara, 128–129, 132

Mashinini, Emma, 165

Mass Democratic Movement, 119

Matanzima, Kaiser, 38–41, 62

Matthews, Z.K., 37–38

Matyolo, Reverend, 27–28, 34

Mazingi, Chief, 66–67

Mbekela, Ben, 18–19, 23

Mbekela, George, 18–19, 23

Mbekeni, Garlick, 46

Mbeki, Govan, 36, 81, 92, 94, 171

Mbeki, Thabo, 137, 171–172, 183

Mbetheni, Wonga, 69

Mdingane, Miss, 21

Meer, Fatima, 40

Mehana, Vukile, 169, 172–173, 179–180, 186

Meiring, Bettie, 136–137

Meiring, Kobus, 136–139

Meiring, Leon, 137–138

Methodist Church
  death of Nelson Mandela, 7, 172–173, 186–187
  Madikizela family, 65–69
  Mandela family, 6, 16–18, 30, 34, 40, 103, 142, 147–150, 154–158, 193–194
  missionaries, 11–19
  M-plan, 59
  opposition to apartheid, 113–115, 148–149
  Pollsmoor Prison, 109–112, 117–118
  Robben Island, 90, 92–93
  University College of Fort Hare, 35, 38

Mfecane, 13, 17

Mfengu tribe, 17

Mhlaba, Raymond, 81, 99, 100

migrant workers, 26

missionaries, 11–15, 36, 191

MK, 77–78, 81, 129, 133–134

Mlambo, Johnson, 115

Mlangeni, Andrew, 81, 99, 100

Mogoba, Stanley, 115–117, 148–149, 156

Mohamed, Nazim, 191

Mokitimi, Seth, 33–34, 113, 148

Moore, Dudley, 109–112, 120

Moore, Ernest, 112

Moral Majority, 105–106

Mostert, Noel, 12

Motsoaledi, Elias, 81

M-plan, 59

Mpofu, Dali, 128

Mpumlwana, Malusi, 179–180, 186

Mqhayi, Krune, 32

Mqhekezweni (Great Place), 23

Mtirara, Justice, 26, 42–43, 45–46, 49, 69

Mtirara, Vulindlela, 156

Mugabe, Robert, 36

Mukherjee, Pranab, 181

Munro, Fred, 100, 103–105, 108

Muslim faith, 92, 95–97, 191

Mvezo (village), 9

NAC, 73–74

Naidoo, M.D., 94

Naidoo, Phyllis, 94

National Action Council, see NAC

Naudé, Beyers, 133

Ndungane, Winston Njongonkulu, 82–85, 87

Newsnight program, 124

Ngoboza, Lillian Noshipo, 125

Ngoyi, Lillian, 62

Ngubengcuka, King, 18–19, 30–31

Nguni people, 14–15

Nkabinde, Ellen, 51

Nobel Peace Prize, 113

Nompuku, Reverend, 156

Nongqawuse (prophetess), 14

Nyobole, Vido, 173–174, 180, 183–184, 186, 192

Obama, Barack, 181

Omar, Dullah, 151, 166–167

Omar, Farida, 151
Orlando West, 53

PAC, 71–72, 82–84, 115
Pan-African Freedom Movement of East
    and Central Africa, 79
Pan Africanist Congress, *see* PAC
pass laws, 71, 83
Pato, Chief, 14
Piliso, headman, 45–46
Piliso-Seroke, Joyce, 165
poetry, 36
Pollsmoor Prison, 96, 99
Potgieter, Pieter, 143
praise-singer (*imbongi*), 32–33, 69
Presbyterian Church, 35
prison warders, *see* warders
private, Nelson Mandela's view that
    religious beliefs are, 3–5, 121, 129, 192

Qunu (village), 16, 23, 182

Ramaphosa, Cyril, 125, 184
religious institutions, *see* church
    organizations
Republic of South Africa, establishment of,
    74
Rivonia Trial, 2, 81
Rivonia trialists, 86–87, 91, 93, 95, 99
Robben Island, 2–3, 9, 80–86, 99, 126
Roman Catholic Church, *see* Catholic
    Church
Rousseff, Dilma, 181
Russell, Philip, 101, 105–106, 108–109

SACC, 92, 115, 132–134, 149
SACP, 3, 69, 112
SAIC, 55
Sakharov Prize, 153
Sarili, Chief, 14
Scholtz, John, 113–118, 167
Seipei, Stompie, 119
Sephton, A.C., 107–108

September, Brother, 89
Seyina, wife of Chief Mazingi, 67
Sharpeville massacre, 71–72
Shaw, William, 11–15, 27, 30, 147, 155
Sidelsky, Lazer, 47–48
Silvester, Victor, 37
Sisulu, Albertina, 52, 125–126
Sisulu, Alice Manse, 70
Sisulu, Walter, 46–48, 52, 62, 81, 89, 95,
    99–100, 125–126, 185
Siwa, Ziphozihle, 175–177, 179, 184–186,
    191
Sobukwe, Robert, 36, 71, 82–84
South African Communist Party,
    see SACP
South African Council of Churches,
    see SACC
South African Indian Congress,
    see SAIC
Sparks, Allister, 184
sport, 37–38
states of emergency, 103, 107
Stevens, Richard J., 107
Stofile, Arnold, 137
Storey, Peter, 90–93, 148–149, 168–169
Student Christian Association, University
    College of Fort Hare, 35, 39
Suduke Methodist mission station, 69
Sunday Times, 105–106
Suppression of Communism Act, 58
Susa, Donovan, 135
Swanepoel, Freek, 144

Tambo, Oliver, 36, 39–40, 61, 79, 115,
    133–134, 153–154, 171
Tennyson, Alfred, 36
Thembu tribe, 9–10, 22, 30, 39, 69, 153
thetha, 182
Thomas, Cal, 103–107
Timm, Derrick, 90
traditions vs religion, 13, 27, 32–34, 66, 68
TRC, 6–7, 113, 133, 149, 166–169
Treason Trial, 65–66, 70, 73

Truth and Reconciliation Commission,
  see TRC
Tshwete, Steve, 137
Tutu, Desmond
  death of Nelson Mandela, 183–186
  opposition to apartheid, 113, 133
  relationship with Nelson Mandela, 4,
    123–127, 158–166, 190, 192–193
  on Thabo Mbeki, 171
  TRC, 6–7, 166–167
Tutu, Leah, 163–165
Tutu, Mpho, 164–165

Umkhonto we Sizwe, *see* MK
UNISA, 47, 51
United Free Church of Scotland, 35
United Nations, 72, 80
University College of Fort Hare, 35–36,
  41–42
University of South Africa, *see* UNISA
University of the Witwatersrand, 52, 61

Vearey, Jeremy, 129–132
Verwoerd, Hendrik, 74
Victor Verster Prison, 118
Villa-Vicencio, Charles, 3–4, 107
Vlok, Adriaan, 133

warders
  Pollsmoor Prison, 101–102, 116–117
  Robben Island, 82–85, 90–92
Washington National Cathedral, 192
Washington Times, 103–107, 110
Waterwitch, Robbie, 134
Weekly Mail, 110
Wellington, Arthur, 33–34
Wesley House (student residence), 38
Wesley, John, 93
Wiggett, Harry, 4, 100–102, 105–109,
  120–121
Williams, Coline, 134
wine for Holy Communion, in prison,
  94–95, 101–102
Winfrey, Oprah, 183
Witkin, Sidelsky and Eidelman (law firm),
  47, 54–55
World Alliance of Reformed Churches, 113
World Council of Churches, 115, 133, 140

Xhoma family, 50–51
Xhosa people, history of, 9–10, 12–17
Xhosa Wars, 9
Xuma, A.B., 48

Zuma, Jacob, 174–175, 180, 184